POWER Optimism

Enjoy the Life You Have
Create the Success You Want

Dana Lightman, Ph.D.

POWER Optimism, LLC

2464 Lafayette Avenue

Abington, PA 19001

215-885-2127

www.poweroptimism.com

Copyright © 2004 by Dana Lightman, Ph.D.

Book Design by Peggy Pfeiffer | BadDog Design

Library of Congress Control Number: 2004093406

ISBN 0-9755419-0-0

I dedicate this book to my husband, Jules,
Whose love and encouragement are unending and unconditional,
And to my family and friends
For helping me to realize my potential and believe in myself.

TABLE OF CONTENTS

OVERVIEW OF THE POWER OPTIMISM SYSTEM

STEP ONE: RELEASE NEGATIVE PATTERNS

Limiting beliefs—A negative perception that you believe to be true and accurate about yourself, others or the world.

Past events—Past incidents that continue to affect how you understand and interpret current situations.

Schemas—An operating system, or mind-program, which affects how your brain filters and processes information it receives.

Emotional hijacks—Overwhelming negative emotions that prevent you from thinking clearly or reacting objectively to events and situations.

STEP TWO: CREATE POSITIVE PRACTICES

Proactive—What can I do?
- Actively choosing responses
- Maintaining personal accountability
- Setting and achieving goals

Open-minded—What are innovative responses?
- Searching out possibilities
- Thinking expansively
- Solving problems creatively

Well-informed—What do I need to know?
- Appraising information objectively
- Using both reason and intuition
- Taking intentional risks

Evolving—What can I learn?
- Rehearsing new life scripts
- Finding growth-promoting insights
- Utilizing self-acceptance

Resilient—What is a motivating interpretation?
- Adopting a positive outlook
- Regulating emotions
- Finding meaning in adversity

1

Preparing the Soil

Chapter One

From Roots to Shoots—The POWER Optimism System

A planted acorn becomes an oak tree due to its life force and energy.
Similarly, each of us is born with a life force that spurs us to grow and
become who we are meant to be. POWER Optimism works in conjunction
with your life energy, strengthening your roots and keeping you grounded,
stimulating the growth of new shoots and the development of new branches
that form your life, energizing the creation that is you.

Truth be told, I never really wanted to write this book. I am more comfortable in the realm of the spoken word: a teacher, therapist, facilitator, trainer, coach, motivational speaker. All jobs that rely on some form of oral communication. But after being asked repeatedly by audience members or workshop participants for a book on POWER Optimism, I finally succumbed and started writing. Just at the point when I was starting to get overwhelmed by the project, rationalizing that the world probably didn't need yet another book telling people how to create success and well-being in their lives, I ran into a participant from one of my early workshops. Like all the people whose stories you'll read, I have changed her name. Let's call her Jane. Here's what she told me:

"I took your POWER Optimism class in the spring of 2002. At that time, my life was an utter mess. I was going through a terrible divorce, had severe financial problems, hated my job, and felt physically and emotionally unhealthy. I was anxious and depressed, and had felt more helpless and sad than I ever had before. When I decided to take POWER Optimism, I thought I could learn something, but I never expected my entire life to change as a result.

Learning about POWER Optimism's Five Practices was a complete awakening for me, and the steps seemed so clear and easy. After the first class, I was so energized that I started to change my outlook by implementing POWER Optimism in my life, beginning with the Proactive Practice. The next Practices simply fell into place and I became Open-minded, Well-informed, Evolved and Resilient. Each Practice complements the others.

For example, I changed the way that I reacted to my divorce. Instead of feeling resentful, I looked for the lessons that were being presented to me. I consciously decided to be Open-minded and asked myself, "What can I learn about myself from this situation?" Of course, I still felt sadness that accompanies divorce, but it no longer overpowered me. I wasn't helpless anymore. Instead, I worked through my emotions, knowing that I was strong enough to handle them and that better things would come into my life. Three months after your class, my divorce was finalized. I feel sure that the months leading up to that would have been disastrous for me if I hadn't been introduced to POWER Optimism.

I truly believe that POWER Optimism changed the course of my life. By incorporating the strategies of POWER Optimism into all aspects of my life, it became impossible for me to continue living "negatively." Instead of feeling like a victim, I took charge of my life, changed my pessimistic outlook and set new goals for myself. I decided to go back to school and pursue a new career as a massage therapist. I began to eat healthily and exercise regularly. Now, I feel great and have lost 10 pounds. I am more financially stable and, although I am not entirely debt-free, I know one day I will be. Finally, I am in a wonderful relationship.

Overall I am happy; I feel freer. I always look to the positive. I know that, although I can't control what happens in my life, I can control my reactions to it. By staying positive, the hardships that occur don't seem so overwhelming. I look at the lessons to be learned as gifts, and know that life is truly wonderful!"

I was bowled over by Jane's story. I am committed to POWER Optimism because the system works, and I am passionate about getting the word out. Jane made me see the necessity of reaching a wider audience and reinforcing my talks and presentations with this book. She spurred me to finish the project. Thank you, Jane.

YOU CHOOSE YOUR ATTITUDE

The principle behind POWER Optimism is simple, but profound. *You* create the thoughts, feelings and actions that affect your life, and *you* have the power to change them to make your life happier and more successful. How? By changing the way you interpret—or understand—the events that happen in your life.

People who interpret the events in their lives based on a *negative* perspective eventually get stuck in fear, sadness and anger. They start expecting the worst in every situation and, more often than not, they find it. They stagnate, and stop growing. On the other hand, people who use a *positive* attitude to evaluate situations become *more* open—things seem more possible, more feasible. They learn, grow and change. This is because our attitudes and our moods are a combination of thoughts, feelings and actions. You've probably experienced this for yourself just going about your life. Think about how, when you're in a bad mood, you are more likely to have negative thoughts and feelings. You may find yourself becoming defensive, snappish and short-tempered. Everything seems awful. If another driver cuts your car off, you might get enraged and yell at him for being so impatient and rude.

On the other hand, when you are in a good mood, your thoughts, feelings and behaviors are, correspondingly, more positive. You feel cheerful, creative and generous. When you're in a good mood and a car cuts you off, you probably shake your head, laugh at how important some people think they are and simply watch the other driver go on his way.

POWER Optimism helps you learn how to choose interpretations that encourage your best and strongest self, interpretations that will unlock your potential and allow you to thrive. Here's how it works: like preparing the earth for planting by removing rocks, pulling weeds and tilling the soil, POWER Optimism teaches you to recognize and eliminate interpretations that are negative, destructive and invalidating. Once the soil is ready, you can plant the seeds for optimism. There are five positive Practices that need to take root for you to become a POWER Optimist, and this book will teach you strategies for planting the seeds of your optimism. After you use the tools to prepare the soil and plant the seeds in your garden, you will learn skills to successfully nurture and maintain the growth of optimism.

CREATING POSITIVE CHANGE AND PERSONAL GROWTH

POWER Optimism grew out of my work as a therapist and my research on how well widows and widowers were doing two and more years after their spouses died. While doing this research, I realized that some people, after grieving, actually became emotionally stronger and more competent than they had been before their spouses passed away. What was consistent among those who experienced personal growth was the trait of *optimism*; they had an approach to life that enabled them to move forward, even though they had been through a very depressing and difficult experience when their spouse died.

The majority of clients I have worked with over the years entered therapy looking for this—the possibility of personal growth and positive change in their lives, despite difficult situations. Similar to the grieving widowed adults, most of my clients began therapy in a period of crisis, depression or intense dissatisfaction with their lives. The method I use, POWER Optimism, enables my clients to heal from old hurts and wounds, and, more than that, to gain control over their lives and unleash their unique potential. POWER Optimism came out of my work with real people who are dealing with very real lives.

POWER Optimism is a system of thinking,
feeling and behaving that creates conditions
for success and promotes a sense of well-being.

The principles of POWER Optimism can help you stay rooted in the present moment so you can enjoy what you're doing and appreciate what you have. It can also help you recognize and use your *growing edge*, the place where you are learning, changing and evolving. A person's growing edge is very much like the new shoots that emerge from the ground in the spring, bringing with them a harvest of vines, flowers and blooms. In the same way, POWER Optimism can help you cultivate and enhance your growing edge to maximize your appreciation and enjoyment of life.

WHAT WE KNOW ABOUT OPTIMISM

The positive attitude I mentioned above is the foundation of *optimism*, the tendency to expect the best possible outcome and focus on the most hopeful aspects of a situation. The more optimistic you are, the more success and well-being come into your life because your thoughts, feelings and actions all work together to generate positive experiences and opportunities. Being in a positive mood (one of the characteristics of optimism) allows a person to be more hopeful and to focus on more options in life. It is an entirely different way of thinking than being in a negative, or pessimistic, mood.

Research shows that optimists live longer and stay healthier as they age. If you keep a positive attitude about aging, you can extend your life by seven and a half years, and you can "age successfully." Aging successfully means staying vital longer and enjoying life because you have the ability to be flexible, adaptable and creative. When compared to people who describe themselves as pessimists, optimists recover faster from surgery, have lower blood pressure and a better immune system. Numerous studies, including those involving individuals with heart disease and cancer, have shown that your state of mind has a strong impact on your healing and ultimate survival. The more optimistic you are, the more of a safeguard you have against depression and anxiety.

Optimists also experience greater success in work and school. Workplace studies indicate that optimists make sound managerial decisions, have better customer relations, come up with creative solutions to problems, and connect with organizational goals. In school settings, optimism is linked to success. In one study of 500 incoming freshmen, optimism predicted their first year grades better than their SAT scores, high school grades or achievement tests. Essentially, optimism reflects how well you feel you can perform. If you feel you can meet the challenges that face you, then you will.

Optimism is also good for relationships. Researchers who have looked at happily married couples find that positive perspectives and interpretations of events strengthen relationships. Happy couples focus on the best in their partners. They give each other credit and praise and look on the bright side. Most importantly, happy couples have what are called "positive illusions" about their spouses, believing in their partner's best assets and expecting the best as well. In turn, partners appreciate this credit and attempt to live up to the "positive illusion." The result is a reinforcement of affection and commitment. On the other hand, when two people who view the world negatively are paired, they tend to use pessimistic explanations of their partner's behaviors. They expect the worst, and often they get it.

No pessimist ever discovered the secret of the stars,
or sailed to an uncharted land
or opened a new doorway to the human spirit.
—Helen Keller

Dr. Martin Seligman, a noted researcher and proponent of optimism, did some of the first research on the effects of an optimistic outlook. He had the idea that success was based not only on intelligence and motivation, but also on optimism. He tested this theory at Met Life, the insurance agency. In insurance, you do a lot of cold calling and get nine rejections for every one person who might be interested in the insurance you're selling. It can be a very discouraging business. Met Life wanted to find out how to help their staff be more effective at selling insurance and learn how they could identify and hire the best salespeople for this tough job.

Dr. Seligman looked at the sales staff and found that those who were more optimistic were the least likely to quit in their first year; they also made more sales. Next, Dr. Seligman had Met Life hire 1,500 salespeople, half of whom had tested as optimists, half of whom had tested as pessimists. The group included 129 people who normally wouldn't have been hired based on their skills; they were accepted this time because they had tested as being *very* optimistic. This group was nicknamed "The Special Forces." Over the next two years, Seligman looked at the sales records of these insurance brokers, and found amazing results. The first year, the optimists outsold the pessimists by 8 percent; the second year, they outsold the pessimists by 31 percent. That was interesting enough, but The Special Forces' results were completely unexpected. The Special Forces outsold the pessimists by 21 percent their first year, and by 57 percent the second year! They even outsold Met Life's regular sales force. Seligman concluded that they did better because they were persistent, motivated and able to deal creatively with challenges and rejection. These are all traits of an optimist. Optimism helped them achieve at their demanding and often discouraging jobs.[1]

The pessimist sees difficulties in every opportunity.
The optimist sees opportunity in every difficulty.
Winston Churchill

Another thing we know is that optimists recover better from failure than pessimists do. In another research study, optimists and pessimists were given slower times in athletic events, thereby making them experience defeat. What's interesting is that the next time they were tested or competed in the athletic events, the optimists tried harder and did better. The pessimists did worse than they had the first time around. The artificial experience of defeat had motivated the optimists, but derailed the pessimists. Seligman notes that pessimists are, overall, "up to eight times more likely to become depressed when bad events happen; they do worse at school, sports and most jobs than their talents augur; they have worse physical health and shorter lives; (and) they have rockier interpersonal relations."[2]

We'd all love to be healthier; age more gracefully; do better in sports, school and work; and realize our full potential, but we're not all innately optimistic. Some of you may be saying to yourselves, "This is hopeless—I'm not an optimist and I can't become one just by wanting it to be so." Others of you may be optimistic most of the time, but don't know what to do when those inevitable down times strike. Some people are optimistic in certain situations, but don't know how to transfer that optimism to circumstances in which they feel negative, hopeless or powerless. The good news is, optimism is not something that's determined at birth. Surprising as it seems, optimism *can* be learned and improved. The POWER Optimism system will show you how.

How is it possible that we can become more optimistic? Well, optimism is a personality trait, a part of each person's unique and individual *temperament*. Your temperament is your normal and natural way of behaving and responding to the world. Other temperamental traits include shyness, extroversion, introversion, impulsiveness and expressiveness. Temperament is created by a combination of our genes and our environment. We used to think that the part of a person's temperament that was caused by genes was immutable, and couldn't be changed or influenced, but we know now that inherited traits can be affected by the surroundings in which a person grows up and learns. We also used to think that the brain stopped growing by the time we reached adulthood. Now we know there are "uncommitted cells" in our brain, and these cells can grow in adulthood. In other words, our brains are always growing and changing, no matter what our age.

This means that you *can* learn how to be more optimistic, regardless of your original personality. Your brain can adjust the way it functions. It's like a runner who is training to complete a marathon or a musician learning a new sonata. With practice, the athlete and the pianist can reach their goals. In the same way, you can train yourself to become an optimist by practicing the strategies of POWER Optimism. It takes time and effort, but you can learn to interpret your life in ways that will increase your happiness and potential. The POWER Optimism system is designed to show you how.

THE FIVE PRACTICES—TAPPING INTO YOUR POWER

POWER Optimism is based on five Practices, which form the acronym POWER. We'll spend a lot more time on these later in the book. I just want to introduce them now, so you'll understand the framework of the system. Each is paired with a question that speaks to the root of the Practice. The five Practices and their accompanying questions are:

- *Proactive—What can I do?* The POWER Optimist who finds him or herself in a difficult or challenging position asks this question to generate actions, rather than passively accepting a bad situation.

- *Open-minded—What are innovative responses?* If you don't try something innovative, you're bound to end up using the same responses you always have, and you are likely to get the same (possibly disappointing) results.

- *Well-informed—What do I need to know?* The process of answering this question includes both gathering information that could bear on the situation and thinking about ways to use the information productively.

* *Evolving—What can I learn?* There is always room for growth and development. By trying out new behaviors and learning from them, you can create positive changes in your life.

* *Resilient—What is a motivating interpretation?* No one goes through life without dealing with crises, challenges, chaos, anger and frustration. If you can't find a motivating interpretation that keeps you going, you are likely to give up.

POWER Optimism is a "co-creative process." This means that you have to use the Practices and incorporate them into your life. It means that you have to take active steps to make your life the way you want it to be. It is not enough to just trust and hope that things will work out—you will have to generate possibilities, recognize opportunities when they arise and act on them. Here's a story, often heard in Alcoholics Anonymous (AA) and other 12-Step programs, that illustrates this point:

Once upon a time, there was a man who was deeply faithful. One day, a huge storm hit the man's town and the nearby river started to rise. Other people started packing up their belongings and fleeing to higher ground to avoid the flood. But the man stayed at home, not even bothering to pack his bags, because he knew that God would take care of him.

The water rose and rose until it crept under the doors of his house and in through his windows. A fire truck drove by and the firefighters shouted out to the man, "It's too dangerous—you can't stay there! Get in the truck!"

The man said, "No, God is going to take care of me!" Soon, the water was waisthigh, and the streets were completely underwater. People paddled by in boats piled high with suitcases and boxes. A Coast Guard boat came by the man's house and the crew yelled out to him, "Swim out to us and climb aboard!"

The man yelled back, "No, go on. God will take care of me!" The rain kept pouring down until the man's entire house was flooded and the water was up to the ceilings. The man clambered onto his roof. A helicopter flew overhead and the pilot spotted the man praying on his roof, surrounded by water. Lowering a rope ladder, the pilot yelled down to the man through a bullhorn, "You down there—grab the ladder and I'll get you to safety!" Again, the man refused, proclaiming that God would take care of him.

Finally, the water rose above the roof entirely, the man had nothing to cling to, and so he drowned. When he arrived at the Pearly Gates, the man was very angry and felt completely betrayed. "My God," he complained, "I put my faith in you and prayed that you would rescue me. I counted on you to rescue me because you told me you would always take care of me. But, when I needed you the most, and my life was in danger, you weren't there!"

God replied, "What do you mean? I sent you a fire truck, a boat, and a helicopter. What more did you want?"

Now, you may believe that the fire truck, boat and helicopter were sent by God, Goddess, the Universe, a Higher Power or the Coast Guard. In any case, the point of the story is that you have to use the tools that are provided to you! In thinking about the Five Practices, the POWER Optimists who found themselves in the middle of that flood would ask:

- *What can I do?* Get into the truck. *(Proactive)*
- *What are innovative responses?* Pass up the fire truck, but make sure another escape route is available, just in case. *(Open-minded)*
- *What do I need to know?* The river may flood and so I should pay attention to rising water levels. *(Well-informed)*
- *What can I learn?* I can balance the possible loss of property with possible gains, such as the opportunity for remodeling or rebuilding my home. *(Evolving)*
- *What is a motivating interpretation?* I can survive a crisis, such as a flood, and it will make me more confident in the face of other crises. *(Resilient)*

ROOTING OPTIMISM IN REALITY

Now, I can already hear the criticism... "This is all wishful thinking! Optimistic thinking can't just be dreamt up so easily. Anyway, it's an unrealistic way of looking at life. Some things are bad, and there's nothing that can be done about it." This common objection reflects the many misconceptions that exist about optimism, as well as confusion about unhealthy kinds of optimism.[3] Optimism is misused when it involves denial—the refusal to acknowledge painful realities and truths. Unhealthy and unrealistic optimism usually come up when people expect things to work out for the best—regardless of what they themselves do, or whether they have made any plans to achieve their goals. People also hide behind inappropriate forms of optimism as a way to avoid pain and growth. This behavior comes out of the mistaken belief that how you live your life is controlled by external events: other people, fate or luck. It's important not to confuse POWER Optimism with these distorted kinds of thinking that aren't really healthy at all. Here are some maladaptive kinds of optimism and an overview of how they differ from POWER Optimism.

Pollyanna Optimism: People who have an unrealistically blind faith that everything will work out regardless of what they do are called "Pollyannas." The name comes from the main character in Eleanor H. Porter's 1912 book, *Pollyanna*, about a girl who always cheerfully saw the good in life. A Pollyanna assumes that things will always be OK. She'll refuse to acknowledge that some things are unpleasant, some experiences are negative and some outcomes undesirable. A Pollyanna optimist might act like he or she is totally fine when he or she has just been dumped by their boyfriend or girlfriend or lost out on a great career opportunity or been unfairly criticized at work.

In the story, Pollyanna was a young girl whose mother had passed away when she was little and her father was also dying. Her father said, "Pollyanna, when I die, I don't want you to feel sad. I want you to play the Glad Game. If you play the Glad Game, you'll know that I'm in Heaven with your mother and I'm happy, and you'll be happy too." Now, Pollyanna really needed my services as a therapist, because when her parents had both died, the worst thing in the world for Pollyanna to do was to pretend to be happy and play the Glad Game. This was a time when it was appropriate, and even necessary, to go through the grieving process and mourn her parents' deaths.

POWER Optimists know that bad things happen and that, while they can't be sugar-coated, these things are survivable. POWER Optimists are resilient in the face of inevitable setbacks and search for creative solutions to life's challenges. POWER Optimists allow themselves to really feel their emotions and to understand them.

Passive Optimism: Passive optimists are a lot like Pollyannas because they think that everything will be OK. Passive optimists specifically believe that the outcome will be due to external factors rather than their own efforts, and so they don't act at all or make any effort. Passive optimists might show up for a public speaking engagement without having prepared any remarks, thinking they'll be able to "wing it." Students who fail to study for exams, or who put off researching their term paper, are being passive optimists. Here's a story about a passive optimist:

A guy named Joe found himself in dire trouble. His business had gone bust, and he was in serious financial debt. He was so desperate that he decided to ask God for help. He prayed, "God, please help me—I've lost my business and if I don't get some money soon, I'll lose my house as well. Please help me win the lottery so I can make everything OK again." Lottery night came, but some other lucky soul won the money. Joe prayed again, "God, please let me win the lottery! I've lost my business, and my house, and I'll lose my car next if something doesn't happen!" Lottery night comes, and again, Joe still has no luck. He prays one more time, "God, why have you forsaken me? I have lost everything I own. Please just let me win the lottery this next time!" Suddenly, there is a blinding flash of light, and the Heavens open. Joe is confronted by God, himself, who says, "Joe, meet me half way on this one... Buy a lottery ticket!"

POWER Optimists know that they are active participants in creating their own successes, and they work on setting personal goals and maintaining accountability. They know that positive thinking must be connected with proactive action in order to be effective... just thinking that something will be OK isn't going to do it.

Dogmatic Optimism: People who ignore signs that things aren't going well are called "dogmatic optimists." They don't pay attention to reality and, instead, imagine outcomes that are not based on the facts. They often fail to prepare or adjust their thinking when things don't work out. An example would be someone who's had several poor performance reviews but who still thinks her position is secure.

A friend of mine, Sheila, decided that she would like to run a half-marathon—that's 13 miles. Sheila is 50 years old and hadn't run a race since she was in her 20's, but she was determined to succeed. She created a training program and started running. The first week, she had run for a couple of miles when her calves and knees started hurting. When she limped home, her husband said, "I'm not sure if this is really right for you. You're in so much pain." Sheila reacted badly and yelled at her husband, "Stop being so negative! Whenever I want to start something new, you're always so negative."

Sheila kept up her running, but her knees and legs hurt more and more. By the second week, she wasn't able to stick with her training program as consistently as she'd have liked. She mentioned this to a co-worker who was a long-time runner, and he showed her a magazine article about conditioning. The article said that new runners (and experienced runners trying to reach a new goal) absolutely have to condition themselves in order to be able to succeed without injury. Sheila didn't like that news either, because it would mean delaying her goal of running that upcoming half marathon in order to build up her strength through conditioning. She said, "I don't care what anyone says. I'm going to do this my own way!"

What is happening here? Sheila was ignoring a wealth of information—not only from her body, which was telling her it was suffering, but also from people who cared about her and had information that could have helped her be successful. So what happened? Four weeks into her training, Sheila went running, even though she was hurt and tired. She tripped, fell and broke her ankle. An ambulance took Sheila to the hospital, where she got a cast on her foot. When

I went to see her, she said, sadly, "See, whatever I try, it doesn't work out. Things never work out for me."

That's dogmatic optimism. There was nothing wrong with Sheila's trying to do something new and fun—far from it! The problem came in when Sheila ignored information from her body and from other people that could have helped her reach her goal. She refused to reassess her goals or her plans for reaching them, and so she failed. POWER Optimists, conversely, take into account all the information that will affect a given situation. They use data, feedback, evidence and information to see how things are going and to make any needed corrections to their plan of action. POWER Optimists keep things in proportion and know that negative information (information that contradicts the information you would prefer to get) may be, in fact, the *precise* information they need. Negative information can help you to reassess what you're doing and help suggest new and different ways to reach your goals.

Irrational Optimism: Some people so firmly believe that everything will turn out all right that they throw caution to the wind and don't assess risks very accurately. These folks haven't really accepted that bad things happen, and they have failed to take sensible, rational precautions that would minimize failure and maximize success. They ignore the old saying, "An ounce of prevention is worth a pound of cure."

My father is a volunteer for SCORE—Senior Core of Retired Executives, an organization sponsored by the Small Business Administration. The mission of SCORE is to bring together retired business owners and executives to share their expertise and knowledge with individuals interested in starting or improving small business enterprises. My father feels that SCORE counselors help people improve their chances of success by grounding them in reality. Lots of people make the mistake of thinking they can be successful without paying attention to the basics. Some people come in to see him without a business plan and with no idea of the competition. Others dream of owning a business in an industry they've never worked in and know nothing about. They just think that they'd like the work—that's like watching Cheers and deciding you want to own a bar! My dad says people come to him with an idea that all their friends say is great and will be a sure hit, so they assume their business will be successful. An irrational optimist expects that things will work out, and often fails to do his or her homework. It's irrational just to rely on passion and excitement without also doing some planning.

The truth is that having a dream and enthusiasm isn't enough. Although 80 percent of new businesses fail within five years, almost all of these failures—some 90 percent—are due to bad business decisions that could have been prevented with planning (like making sure there's enough short-term capital to keep the business going if times get tough). The Small Business Administration says that "starting and managing a business takes motivation, desire and talent. It also takes research and planning." People who want to start a business need to have good ideas about what their business will do, what their business goals are, how they will be better than their competitors and what their marketing strategies will be.[4]

Actually, like starting a small business, achieving our dreams requires a firm footing in reality. POWER Optimism is based on reality. POWER Optimists work to make well-informed decisions and take risks based on accurate information. To create success, they know that they have to do a lot of leg work, thinking and planning. POWER Optimists set realistic and well-informed goals, and then work to achieve them.

Wishful Optimists: These people are so convinced that things will come out for the best that they focus on unattainable goals or fail to actively work towards even realistic goals. They are often let down when their dreams fail to come true even though they haven't really thought through how they were going to turn their dream into reality.

In the picture below, the cow is saying: "I give chocolate milk!" The chicken next to her is saying "I lay golden eggs!" Now, we all know that's not possible. Cows don't give chocolate milk, and chickens don't lay golden eggs, regardless of how much they wish they did. Those are examples of wishful optimism, hoping for things that are not going to happen.

Here's a story relayed to me by a participant at one of my workshops. It illustrates how to achieve your dreams by letting go of impossible wishes and focusing on attainable goals. Mark was an older man who loved ice hockey. If he could have any job in the world, he would love to be a professional hockey player and be a star in the National Hockey League, but he had grown up in Florida, where ice-skating wasn't very popular, and he never learned to skate when he was a kid. He did learn when he was older and lived in Chicago, where hockey and skating are much more common, but by then it was too late. You have to start early if you want to be a major league hockey player, and he hadn't had the chance.

Mark watched hockey on TV and went to the local team's games, and he could have become bitter about his lost dreams and opportunities, but Mark is a POWER Optimist. Instead, one day when he was at a Blackhawks' game, he started talking with a guy sitting near him. He and Mark really hit it off, and before long the man was telling Mark about his job as the coach for the local high school hockey team.

As a result of this conversation, Mark started volunteering with the high school team. He discovered that he got a lot of satisfaction from being part of a team, helping the players and becoming knowledgeable about the game's intricacies. He's now an assistant coach, still loving every minute of his involvement with the high school team. Mark's not a star player for the NHL, and he never will be, but he is very happy and satisfied with the way that the game he loves is a bigger part of his life, and the fact that he is a part of the local hockey community.

POWER Optimists set achievable goals. Their hopes are focused on what they can accomplish, while developing their best abilities. POWER Optimism can't make the cow give chocolate milk, the chicken lay the golden egg or Mark play in the NHL. Some things just aren't possible. POWER Optimism does, however, give you the tools to make your vision *take form* in a way that's in sync with reality and with who you are. It helps you create your own form of golden eggs or hockey stardom. POWER Optimists hold on to their vision, but let go of the form that it will take in reality.

YOU CREATE YOUR SUCCESS

POWER Optimism can help you to be your best person possible, to energize the potential that is uniquely *your own*. You will learn that your thoughts and feelings and actions don't have to be reactive. You can be an active creator of your life and actually change what happens to you. POWER Optimism will give you the strategies and tools to choose thoughts, feelings and actions that are productive, that focus on positive outcomes and that create success and well-being. The program is a beneficial and empowering way to address life's challenges, and produces energy and strength for people who use it.

*You are
an active agent
in how your
life turns out!*

I am not promising the moon and the stars. That's not realistic. No one will experience success and happiness all of the time. POWER Optimism acknowledges that, sometimes, the glass *is* half empty. At the same time, the program is grounded in the belief that dwelling on emptiness is not productive. POWER Optimism helps you to shift your perceptions, so you can see the part of the glass that is actually full. It is only from *recognizing* the truth, and working through painful and difficult times, that we grow and learn. Success often comes out of growth that is spurred on by failure. By using strategies that will encourage success, POWER Optimists become agents of positive growth and change in their own lives.

One of my clients, Tom, came to me for help in coping with a workplace problem that was causing him to feel depressed and powerless. Tom had a troublesome boss who continuously ignored his point of view in assessing difficult situations. This eventually led to a particularly painful incident in which Tom was unfairly blamed for a work infraction. He became more and more anxious about his position and felt unable to meet with his boss about anything. He wanted to quit his job, but felt like he had no viable options. Using POWER Optimism's tools, Tom was able to shift his perspective. He knew that there was a problem in his relationship with his boss, but instead of focusing on his boss, he focused on himself. He discovered ways in which he was contributing to the problem by allowing his insecurities and fears to take over. Tom learned to recognize and redirect his unproductive reactions, to think before acting and to choose beneficial responses. By using this difficult situation as a vehicle for self-discovery, Tom was able to change his relationship with his boss. He now feels effective and competent as he enters his workplace and has taken the initiative in proposing new ideas and projects for his department.

Tom's story highlights how the POWER Optimism system can help you find fresh ways to think about problems in your life and turn disappointments into new opportunities. But POWER Optimism isn't just designed to help you handle problems or difficulties.

I'm such a supporter of POWER Optimism because it can help you change your life by increasing opportunities for pleasure and enjoyment. Here's how I used the five Practices of POWER Optimism to shift my own perspective and create a positive outcome:

The truth is, if I could have anything in the world, I wouldn't be a therapist and motivational speaker. What I really would like to be is ... Meryl Streep. I would *love* to be celebrated for my acting abilities and lauded by both the public and my colleagues. I've worked on my acting a fair amount. I've taken acting lessons, and I've been in several amateur plays at local theaters, but when I thought about how my theatrical "career" was going, and how talented an actress I was, I had to face facts. I had to admit that (like the chicken), I will never attain my "golden egg" dream of being Meryl Streep!

I could think of myself as a failure because I have a desire to be an accomplished actress—and it's not going to happen. That would be an unproductive way of thinking about this situation, because it would add to my negative perceptions and feelings by using a negative interpretation. Here's what happened instead. Using the Proactive Practice, I asked myself, "What can I do to continue to enjoy my love for acting in a way that fits my life and skills?" I chose to continue to take acting lessons, even though I will never become a professional. Although I am a perpetual amateur, I still relish the creativity and challenge of acting classes.

I used the Open-minded Practice to think about innovative ways that I could incorporate my love of acting into my professional work. In leading workshops, I often illustrate concepts with role play. I become a trouble-making employee or a suicidal staff person. The role plays enable participants to experience and practice new learning—and I get to act. Quite often, people come up to me afterwards and say, "You're a really good actress." This is my version of winning the Oscar!

I have many strengths and talents, but I am just not a good enough actress to support myself that way. This is the *Well-informed Practice*, assessing information objectively. When I thought about my acting career, and truthfully answered the question "What do I need to know?" the response was that I would not be able to make a living as a professional actress. While I enjoyed acting classes, and relished my opportunities to role play in workshops, this just wasn't enough. I could keep feeling dissatisfied and frustrated, but I decided to find a new course of action.

I thought about what it is about acting that I find appealing; what components of the acting experience bring me joy? I used the *Evolving Practice* and sought out what I could learn from the situation. I figured out that I like being in front of a group of people, holding their attention, and building their enthusiasm. I get energy from that. This insight propelled me to join Toastmasters International, which lets me speak to groups, and also helps me to improve my skills as a presenter. Being a motivational speaker is another way I get to use my love of acting.

I was able to apply the *Resilient Practice* to generate a motivating interpretation that allows me to keep going and to enjoy what I'm doing. Although I will never beat Meryl Streep out for an Academy Award, the ways I get to act make me happy. I held onto the vision of using my acting—by bringing it into my successful professional career—but let go of the form, which was the unrealistic idea that only being a professional actress could satisfy me.

NURTURING YOUR OWN GARDEN

A workshop participant once said, "I am here to avoid Power Pessimism!" This book will show you how you can avoid it, too. The POWER Optimism process is not a one-shot approach to life, something that can be picked up and put down again. Rather, it is a systematic way of changing the way you approach your life. It will require you to revisit the Practices and keep applying their lessons on a regular basis.

We'll spend some time in the next chapter looking at the science behind POWER Optimism and discussing the ways that your thoughts, feelings and actions all affect one another. Then, we'll go through the first step in the POWER Optimism program—identifying your own individual stumbling blocks, your particular negative patterns—and learning ways to overcome them. Finally, we'll focus on the five POWER Practices. There are lots of strategies and ideas in the book, because what works for one person may not feel right to another. If you like something, that's a sign that it's a good strategy for you. If it leaves you cold, use a different one. Take what works for you, and don't worry about the things that don't connect for you. It will also be helpful to read sections of the book repeatedly, and do the exercises more than once. Keep releasing your negative patterns and revisiting the Practices, especially if something is happening in your life that's making you feel stuck, depressed or angry.

Replacing old, unhealthy ways of thinking is not easy, but it is very rewarding. There is no need to be critical or judgmental as you say goodbye to outmoded and unproductive thoughts, feelings and behaviors. I invite you to make your way through this book with a feeling of openness, lightness and possibility for the future. Together, we will discover new insights, uncover new strengths and draw on your own, natural gifts.

> *A tree that reaches past your embrace grows from one seed.*
> *A structure over nine stories high begins with a handful of earth.*
> *A journey of a thousand miles starts with a single step.*
> —*Lao Tsu*

Chapter Two

A Daisy Among the Orchids—
Change Your Perceptions and Change Your Reality

When you plant a garden, you choose the plants and flowers that are pleasing to you.
You arrange them in ways that bring you joy. The garden is beautiful to you
because you decide it is beautiful. Even if someone else doesn't like your garden, it
doesn't matter because you know your garden suits you, fits your vision and fills you
with delight. Grow your life like a garden, filling it with thoughts, feelings
and actions that will produce a fruitful harvest.

Arlene came to see me because she was having trouble in her relationships caused by chronic low self-esteem. These feelings went back to her high school days, when she knew she wasn't as popular as the other girls and hadn't felt like she fit in. Arlene didn't enjoy the same passions that the other girls did—she wasn't that interested in boys and fashion left her cold. While Arlene wasn't without friends, she wasn't one of the "in" crowd of girls, who seemed to live a kind of charmed and magical existence. Now in her forties, Arlene's feelings of inadequacy continued to affect her, particularly at the office. Her work place seemed to her to greatly resemble high school, where youth, popularity and beauty were the most highly prized assets anyone could have.

While Arlene is a lovely person, and is very empathetic and intelligent, she didn't think she was as valued as her co-workers, who she perceived as being more attractive and in demand for lunch dates and after-work activities. Although people really respond to Arlene when she's relaxed, her low self-confidence causes her to clam up and almost vanish when she feels uncomfortable. These habits weren't helping her to shine at work, and made her feel badly about herself. I asked her, if she had to describe the so-called "beautiful people" with whom she worked (and had attended high school), what kind of flower they would be. "Oh, that's easy," she said, "They're orchids." What kind of flower would Arlene say she is? "A daisy," she said glumly.

OK, she's a daisy. What Arlene had to learn was how to appreciate her daisy-ness. There were lots of things that she liked about herself. She just never paid attention to them because they weren't things that were characteristics of orchids. When Arlene started thinking about what she liked about herself, what she was good at, she started appreciating her own unique qualities and attributes. Then, Arlene realized that she didn't want to be an orchid anymore. She liked being who she was—a beautiful daisy. Most of all, she learned that life would be really boring if there were only orchids. It's more interesting to have all kinds of flowers, and daisies are wonderful.

By starting to see herself as a daisy, as something valuable and desirable, Arlene was able to appreciate herself. She stopped criticizing herself for not being an orchid and, in doing so, totally changed how she felt and thought about herself. Because her feelings and thoughts have shifted, she radiates more confidence and acts with more self-assurance. Arlene created a new reality that was not only more realistic, but also more pleasurable. She no longer believes she is not pretty enough or attractive enough; she knows she is a beautiful daisy and she feels great about that. In turn, she is happier at work and has opened up to her colleagues, who are more likely to include her in their plans.

In the scenery of spring
there is nothing superior
nothing inferior
flowering branches
are by nature
some short
some long
　　　　　—Zen proverb

Arlene's story illustrates why your interpretation of the events in your life is so fundamental to creating happiness and success. In this chapter, I'll talk about the role of interpretation in becoming a POWER Optimist. I'll also go over how the brain works and describe the therapeutic model at the heart of POWER Optimism. Finally, I'll introduce the two steps that are the foundation of becoming a POWER Optimist.

TWO SIDES TO EVERY STORY

One of the most interesting findings in modern psychology is that the way people perceive and interpret things affects how they feel about them. As the old saying goes, there are two sides to every story. Now, modern science tells us that the side people see affects what they think, how they feel, and ways they behave. POWER Optimism is based on the fact that you can *choose* which side you see. You can *choose* how to interpret what happens in your life.

Let's look at some images that will illustrate how this works.

Each of these images contains two different pictures: the image may be seen as either one thing or another, two different interpretations of reality. You might see the first image as two faces, looking at one another. Or, you might see it is a curvy vase. The other image can look like a face in shadow, or it can look like someone playing a trumpet. You might see a rabbit in the last picture, or you may be drawn to the picture of the duck. Both images are there; it just can take some work to see them. Can you see both images in each of the pictures? Can you shift your perception back and forth between the two different pictures?

Just as these images have two possible interpretations, the events and circumstances in our lives can be interpreted in many ways. POWER Optimism rests on the fundamental principle that our interpretation of the events and circumstances in our lives is more important than the events themselves. We create interpretations by defining situations, drawing conclusions and making inferences and assumptions. In other words, when we choose an interpretation, we are assigning *meaning* to the event. Here's a story that highlights how this works:

An avid duck hunter was in the market for a new dog. He was dumbfounded when he found a dog that could walk on water to retrieve birds! Certain that his hunting buddy would never believe that he owned such a dog, the man decided to invite his friend out for a day of hunting at a nearby lake and show off the dog's abilities. While they were hunting, a flock of ducks flew by and the hunters raised their guns. A duck fell into the water, and the man's dog jumped in to retrieve the bird, never getting more than his paws wet. The man's buddy watched the dog, apparently uninterested. Finally, the man couldn't stand the silence any more, and he asked his friend, "Did you notice anything unusual about my new dog?"

"Sure did," the friend replied, "your dog can't swim."

Same situation—both men watched the dog walk on water, but they assigned totally different meanings to what the dog had done. Where one man saw miraculous ability, his friend thought the dog was a loser who couldn't swim. Which was accurate? In a sense, they *both* were.

How do you know which interpretation is right for you? Is the picture a vase, or is it two people looking at each other? Is the other image a rabbit or a duck? Is the hunting dog miraculous, or can't he swim? The trick is identifying the interpretation that is *right for you*. Regardless of the bare facts, you can choose an interpretation that will let you grow, change and move forward. Alternatively, you can choose an *interpretation* that will reinforce your worst beliefs and cause you pain. POWER Optimism teaches you how to choose interpretations that enable you to create conditions for success and promote a sense of well-being.

> If we wish to change our sentiments,
> it is necessary before all to modify the idea which produced them,
> and to recognize either that it is not correct itself,
> or that it does not touch our interests.
> —W.E.B. DuBois

Let me give you an example from my own life. When I was 35, I was planning to marry Nick, an Englishman I had been dating for three years. Nick had left the United States and gone back to England, and I moved over there to be with him. I left my job, sold my car, gave up my apartment, got rid of almost all my worldly possessions and flew to London. When I arrived, I found him withdrawn and sullen; he stayed that way for months. Finally, after the tension had become unbearable, Nick blurted out, "I will never marry you because you don't have the perfect body!" Ouch! As a woman who had struggled with weight and self-esteem issues for a long time, I was devastated.

For years afterwards, my interpretation of this event was that Nick was right—I was too fat to be attractive. I chose this interpretation based on *my own* belief that I was undesirable. I had felt this way even before I had gone to England, and my negative self-concept meant that Nick's comment rang true. My beliefs about myself allowed his criticism to stick to me like Velcro® and caused me to choose a painful interpretation that made me feel like a victim.

In order to loosen the grip of this interpretation, I decided to reexamine the event. First, I had to admit that if I hadn't already held negative beliefs about my attractiveness, Nick's comment might have sounded ludicrous rather than believable. Second, I realized that Nick was just not ready to marry me, despite his love for me. Because he lacked the courage to openly admit that he wasn't ready for marriage, he had to be hurtful and cruel to me so that I would make the break he desired. My new interpretation was that Nick attacked my body because he knew it would cause me to end our relationship. His comment succeeded—I did return to the United States the very next week. With this reinterpretation, I was able to see myself as someone who would be attractive and desirable to the right man. I assigned a different meaning to the event, which enabled me to choose a new interpretation that made me feel good about myself.

The truth is, we all have the ability to choose how we perceive situations in life. POWER Optimism gives you the tools and strategies you need to choose interpretations that will let you enjoy your life.

Your interpretation of an event is more important than the event itself.

THOUGHTS, FEELINGS AND BEHAVIORS— AN INTERCONNECTED SYSTEM

POWER Optimism is based on the newest findings about neurology, the science of how the brain works. One important discovery, in terms of human psychology, is that our thoughts, feelings and behaviors are all intertwined.[1] It is as if our brains have neural circuits made up of our feelings and their accompanying thoughts and behaviors. Our reactions are *created* by the brain based on the meaning we assign to the situations that are occurring to us. In other words, our reactions are created by our interpretations.[2]

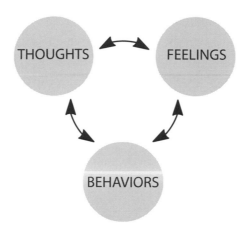

Think about a time when someone said something snippy or mean-spirited to you, and try to remember how you felt. Maybe someone suggested that you needed to lose some weight, weren't the best driver around, had a terrible haircut or were chronically late for appointments. Were you mad? Defensive? Did you want to lash out and tell him what a big jerk he was? Or, maybe the remark didn't make any difference to you one way or the other. You might have brushed off the comment, or laughed about it and not thought about it afterwards. The difference in your reaction is based on your interpretation, the meaning you assigned to the comments. The point is, no one can actually *make* you think, feel or act a certain way. Your reaction could be blasé indifference, amusement, fear or anger—but *you* determine what it will be.

Changing your *interpretation* of an event affects your feelings, thoughts and actions because they all need to work together to make sense of the world. Because feelings, thoughts and actions are all inter-related, changing one affects the others. You can change your thoughts, which will help you change your feelings and how you act. Or, you can change how you act, and that influences how you feel and think. Alternatively, by working on your feelings, you can affect how you think and act. It doesn't matter where you start, since they are all tied in together.

When you are in a bad mood or things seem bleak, what's important is to start working on the aspect of yourself—thought, feeling or action—that is easiest for you. Some people find it easier to work on changing their thoughts; others are more comfortable with changing their feelings or actions. For this reason, POWER Optimism includes a range of strategies so that there's something for everyone.

> *The thing that upsets people is not what happens*
> *but what they think it means.*
> —*Epictetus*

GETTING ON THE UPWARD SPIRAL

Scientists who study the brain suggest that optimistic and pessimistic ways of thinking occur in different parts of the brain and might be driven by different kinds of brain chemistry. In a positive frame of mind, your brain is open to possibilities; it's looking for connections and ideas. This open, energized state is what is called an *upward spiral*. POWER Optimism's goal is to teach you how to produce an upward spiral as much as possible. When you're on an upward spiral, your thoughts, feelings and actions are all working together to create a sense of well-being and opportunities for success. When your feelings, thoughts and actions are all directed positively, they interact and reinforce each other in an intensely powerful way. Best of all, when your thoughts, feelings and actions all work together, you are motivated and stimulated.

Think about times when you really had it together, when everything seemed to be in sync. At moments like this, time flies and everything seems easy. You lose track of the hours and are effortlessly engaged in whatever you're doing. This experience is called *flow* and, when you're in it, you are on an upward spiral. You have the ability to create interesting and energizing ways to manage day-to-day problems and challenges. Your brain is both creating and using positive connections. The goal of the POWER Optimism system is to help you have more moments where everything comes together like this and you're really enjoying life.

How does this feeling of flow connect with the discussion about how your interpretations influence your feelings, thoughts and actions? When you have an experience and make an interpretation that is right for you, you will feel like you're on an upward spiral. The correct interpretation of the external world is the choice or interpretation (for your unique circumstance) that places you on an upward spiral so that you feel expanded and uplifted.[3] A correct interpretation results in your feeling:

- positive
- healthy
- constructive
- creative

- tolerant
- generous
- energized
- flexible

Of course, the reverse is true. Interpretations and choices that *aren't right* for you put you on a *downward spiral*, which is characterized by feeling shut down, lacking energy or depressed. When you make a decision that's not right for you, your brain reinforces old and negative patterns that are not creative and don't lead to new ideas. A decision that is wrong for you is connected to feelings of:

- negativity
- distorted perceptions
- destructiveness
- invalidation
- lethargy

- defensiveness
- self-criticism
- stubbornness
- resistance to change

People often refer to a downward spiral as low energy, depression, a bad mood or other negative physical symptoms. It's probably happened to you. Have you made a decision and felt awful about it? After the decision, you may have gotten a headache, started to feel your stomach churn or had problems sleeping. That's your mind and body's way of saying "something is not right here!" It's important to honor what your body and your unconscious mind are trying to tell you and to learn to pay attention to their signals about the choices you're making. Practicing the principles of POWER Optimism can also help you to raise your self-awareness so that you develop a greater facility in noticing your upward and downward spirals and what moves you along them. With both observation and practice, you can become adept at intervening in your own thoughts, moods and behaviors and in changing the direction of the spiral you are on from down to up.

Crystal, one of my workshop participants, after listening to me describe the difference between a downward spiral of energy and an upward one, shared how she decided to leave her job based on these kinds of feelings. Crystal was a popular high school teacher and had been for 23 years. She was enjoying her summer vacation when she realized that she couldn't do it anymore. The more she thought about returning to her job, the more depressed and frustrated she felt. All the energy seemed to be seeping out of her body. After feeling this way for several weeks, Crystal realized that she had to leave teaching, even though her friends thought she was crazy to give up the secure position she'd had for so long. She was scared, but the month before classes started for the fall, Crystal wrote a letter to her principal and resigned from her job. She felt bad about putting the school in a bind at such short notice, but she went ahead and did what she thought was right for her. She immediately felt better, more energized and cheerful. She had made the correct interpretation for her own unique circumstances, and the correctness of that interpretation was reflected in Crystal's feeling energized. That was five years ago, and she says the time since she quit her job has been the best she's ever had. Crystal honored her feelings about leaving her teaching position and was able to bring greater joy and contentment into her life.

The point of POWER Optimism is to give you additional resources and tools that you can use to create opportunities for success and a sense of well-being, help generate positive interpretations and increase the energy and ideas that are available to you. This does not mean you will never suffer or have anything bad happen to you. That wouldn't be a realistic promise for me to make. What we're shooting for is not a lack of suffering, but a sense of competence and security. Even when something bad happens, you feel confident that you will be able to get through it and that you will grow by facing the difficulty. In other words, POWER Optimism will teach you how to stop a downward spiral from getting out of control, how to move back into an upward spiral and how to keep your energy moving upward to create what you want in your life.

> I taught my children that any situation in life that's negative,
> there is something positive you can do with it.
> "Use the difficulty" it's like a motto in our family.
> —Michael Caine

THE THEORY AND SCIENCE BEHIND POWER OPTIMISM

Many participants in my workshops and classes want to know why POWER Optimism works. One of the reasons the program is so effective is because it is based on the proven therapy practices of cognitive-behavior therapy. POWER Optimism is also rooted in positive psychology, a perspective that focuses on helping clients unleash their full potential and vitality. Plus, the program draws on recent discoveries about how the brain functions to shape our thoughts, emotions and actions. By understanding the theory and science behind POWER Optimism, you will gain a deeper appreciation for the process of change and growth which results from the program.

Cognitive-Behavior Therapy and Positive Psychology

POWER Optimism is based on the principles of "cognitive-behavior therapy," which is now the most common form of talk therapy in the United States. The term "cognitive" comes from the method's emphasis on "cognitions," or thoughts. Cognitive therapy is based on the idea that a person's negative interpretation of events (called "cognitive distortions") gives him or her an inaccurate picture of what's happening in his or her life and may lead to anxiety, depression or anger. Cognitive therapy teaches people to identify these distorted interpretations and replace them with healthier ways of thinking. By changing one's thoughts, people can also alter their feelings and behaviors. The term "behavior" refers to changing unproductive, ineffectual and destructive behaviors. Behavior therapy focuses on replacing unwanted habits with more desirable ones and identifying activities for potential pleasure and mastery.

Research shows that this kind of therapy is very effective in treating anxiety and depression. In fact, cognitive-behavior therapy has been shown in some cases to be as effective as medication. Anti-anxiety medication and anti-depressants are necessary and helpful for some people, and if you think you require medication, it is important to be evaluated to determine an appropriate course of treatment. Studies suggest that medication is most effective in providing long-term improvement when combined with learning techniques to challenge the assumptions and incorrect interpretations that underlie despair, hopelessness and anxiety. Because POWER Optimism draws on both cognitive and behavioral techniques to teach you how to replace negative thought patterns and behaviors with more productive and empowering ones, it can enhance the effectiveness of medication and therapy in shaping a positive perspective and outlook.[4]

POWER Optimism also draws on what is called "positive psychology." This type of psychology concentrates on people's assets rather than their deficits. Instead of focusing on what's wrong with people—on their victimization, their mental illnesses or the characteristics of their depression—positive psychology looks at people's strengths. Its goal is to emphasize positive emotions and moods, not just help people become "not unhappy." Positive psychology and its related models are based on the fact that people want to reach their *optimal potential*, not merely to be "OK" or "less depressed." This kind of therapy helps people to build and enhance the positive character traits of will-power, creativity, courage, gratitude, common sense and cheerfulness.[5]

POWER Optimism builds on positive psychology by offering a way to reach your full potential. POWER Optimism is not about focusing on your faults or analyzing your shortcomings. We all have things about ourselves that aren't perfect, and there will always be things we'd like to change. The heart of this system is to build up your strengths rather than tearing down your weaknesses. When your strengths are working at their best, it will be easier for you to get on an upward spiral and to increase your opportunities for success and well-being.

> *Your own excellence, success and greatest pride*
> *comes from one person, you.*
> —*Frank Robinson*

Pathways in the Brain

What creates negative patterns, like my poor self-concept about my attractiveness? I've talked about how musicians and athletes gain skills by practicing their talents. Repetition builds strength. The brain is the same way: repetitive thoughts, actions and beliefs build patterns in the way we think, feel and act. These *patterns* turn into habits as they become stronger and more ingrained. Sometimes the patterns are good; sometimes they are bad. While repetition in thinking, feeling and acting builds mental habits, it's just as important to know that the opposite is true. A habit can also be *unlearned* and *replaced* with a more effective or useful way of acting and thinking. It's a matter of retraining the brain and replacing old habits with new ones.[6]

As we go through life, our brains are continually absorbing information and making connections between different pieces of information to make sense of what's happening around us. These connections are called "neural pathways" and they guide the brain's activity.

Connections that are used a lot are strengthened. If I have a thought, it triggers the brain to respond. If I have the same thought often, it becomes a pathway in the brain, just like a path through the woods is made smoother the more frequently it's walked on. We get messages from society, from our families and from the media, and these all contribute to our mental pathways. These messages help form our sense of self—our expectations of what is normal and acceptable. Things happen to us and we respond, and this also creates pathways.

Many times, the habituated pathway is helpful. For example, when you're acting in a play, or playing a favorite song, the default mechanism is good because it lets you perform more skillfully. The ingrained habit and learning can take over if you blank out and forget your lines! When you're on "autopilot," your brain is using the default pathways that have been established already.

But people also create negative pathways, and that's not helpful. A negative ingrained habit can prevent someone from responding in a new way to challenges. An ingrained habit can make it hard to think outside the box, to come up with new strategies or to avoid old pitfalls. You know you are trapped using negative pathways when the same bad things keep happening to you in your relationships or at work. This continuous reinforcement of negative interpretations is also known as "repeated episodes" or *repisodes*.

When faced with a new situation, the brain can use the tried and true pathways that have been strengthened everyday, it could try to use pathways that have been ignored and weakened, or it can create new pathways. It's easy to see that the brain will go for the first option, the more familiar pathways. In choosing, the brain strengthens that pathway even more, so that eventually this becomes the default pathway—the one you automatically and immediately apply to all situations. Here's a story about these ideas:

A poor man was walking through the forest, reflecting on his many troubles. He stopped to rest against a tree, which happened to be a magical tree that granted the wishes of those who touched it. The man leaned back and realized that he was thirsty and wanted something to drink. Instantly, a cup of cool water was in his hand. Shocked, he looked at the water and decided to drink it. His thirst quenched, the man realized that he was hungry. Immediately, a feast appeared, spread out before him. "My wishes are being granted," the man thought in disbelief. "Well, then, I wish I had a beautiful home to live in." As soon as the words were out of his mouth, a lovely home appeared in the meadow. A huge smile crossed the man's face as he wished for servants to take care of his every need. When they appeared, he knew he had been somehow blessed by an amazing power, and he wished for an intelligent, beautiful, loving wife to share his good fortune. Snap! She was there. "Wait a minute," the man said to his wife. "I'm not this lucky; this can't happen to me!" As he spoke, everything disappeared: the cup of water, the feast, the house, servants and wife. The man shook his head and sighed, "I knew it." Then he walked away, thinking again about his many troubles.

The poor man in the story had set up and reinforced a pathway that limited what he thought could happen to him. Then he acted in a way that made that belief real. His negative pathway prevented him from imagining good fortune and led him to say, "This can't be happening to me." His windfall vanished and sadness was, once more, his reality. The man's brain had been habituated to make connections that weren't accurate, and didn't serve him well, because he really *was* experiencing good fortune! We are all, like this man, blinded in some way to our own possibilities and our life potential.

POWER Optimism could have helped him. As I said earlier, an ingrained habit that's unhealthy *can be replaced* by a new way of thinking, feeling and behaving. This is true because brain connections and pathways that aren't used get weaker and are eventually lost. Psychologists call this process "extinguishing" because the pathway eventually vanishes. Think about a foreign language that you might have learned in high school, but didn't use after graduation. Eventually, your skill in speaking the language declined and you couldn't remember it very well anymore. In the same way, brain patterns that aren't used regularly will become weaker and diminish.

So, replacing negative patterns involves practicing and reinforcing *new* pathways. As you do this, you're working to extinguish the old pathway so it doesn't continue to trip you up. Eventually, the new and healthy patterns become ingrained, enabling you to respond to life with openness, creativity, flexibility and spontaneity. Once they are strong, the healthy pathways replace the old, negative pathways and become the default pathways for your brain. POWER Optimism helps you to *retrain* your brain and establish new, positive pathways over the old, negative ones.

Think about how I interpreted Nick's nasty comment about my weight. Long before I had even met Nick, I had created a negative pathway that said I was too heavy to be attractive to men. When Nick lashed out, I interpreted his comment using my habituated pathway, one of negative self-image. It took me a long time to realize that I had a *choice* in how to interpret his comment. We all have these pathways and are constantly building some up, while letting others become weaker. When our pathways are set, we stop recognizing that we have choices, that there are other ways to interpret things. We get stuck in the rut of continuously interpreting our lives in unnecessarily negative ways. We imagine the worst, and then make it so by believing in it. When I reinterpreted Nick's comment, I started building a new pathway. The new pathway said I *was* attractive. In time, this pathway replaced my old ways of thinking, and I was much happier and had a more realistic view of myself as a result.

You might say, how can I act a certain way without wanting to? Isn't that fakery? At first, you're right—it's a matter of practice, not habit. You may feel strange acting as if you're optimistic and choosing to make positive interpretations of the things happening around you. It will feel weird initially, but as the habit becomes ingrained, it will get easier and come into sync. I should be clear that I'm not talking about being disingenuous, denying your feelings or not letting others see your real emotions. These types of responses are not helpful for someone who wants to be a functioning and healthy adult. What I'm talking about is your making a conscious, intentional choice to shift your thoughts, feelings and behaviors.

WORKING THE PRINCIPLES OF POWER OPTIMISM

Step One: Identify Negative Patterns

The first step in POWER Optimism is to identify and release negative patterns. You have to *recognize* the negative patterns that have been created and that affect how you interpret the things that happen in your life before you can replace them with new and more productive pathways. Without the hard work of identifying and overcoming the negative patterns, it isn't possible to build new behaviors, thoughts and actions. This is why positive *thinking in and of itself* often fails to serve people well. People who just "decide" they're going to look at things in a more positive way have not figured out *why* their thinking was pessimistic and limiting in the first place, so all their good intentions get overwhelmed by the long-established negative patterns, and they can't make effective changes in their lives. An established negative pattern will always overwhelm and beat out a new, positive thought, *unless and until* the negative pathway has been replaced by a positive one.

Think about it like a garden. You have to prepare a garden before it can bloom. Unless you pull out the old deadwood, clear away the rocks and remove the heavy clay from the garden, there won't be any room for the new healthy growth. The same is true for cultivating optimism. You first have to find the rocks and clay and deadwood— your unique, negative patterns—and remove them. Only then can you nurture positive thoughts, feelings and behaviors—after the negative thinking has been cleared away. Until you've cleared out the garden and nourished the soil, weeds will always overwhelm the flowers' tiny seedlings. In the next chapter, we'll get into the specifics of the four negative patterns that shape the way we interpret the world and prevent us from thinking optimistically. You'll look at which patterns affect you and what you can do to remove them.

Step Two: Create New and Positive Patterns

The second step in POWER Optimism is to replace the negative patterns with positive ones that *encourage optimism*. As I just said, this isn't just a matter of saying "I'm going to be an optimist now!" It takes practice and effort. Step Two involves intentionally planning for, working towards and creating positive practices. Ingraining positive practices and optimism is very much like growing lovely flowers and vegetables in our gardens. You can't just dump a bunch of seeds on the ground and then ignore them for a month or two. They wouldn't grow very well. Instead, you have to help the seeds *grow* by watering them, weeding the garden and being attentive to their needs. The seeds of positivity and optimism also require time, attention and planning. Part Two describes the particular strategies that you can use to encourage optimism in your life to build new, positive practices.

You might be asking yourself, "All this weeding and planting and nurturing the seeds of my personal growth—isn't this a lot of work?" The answer depends—like everything we've been looking at so far—on your interpretation. Yes, it takes work, but I prefer to view the work and effort as the energy that fuels an exciting adventure: my life. I do the work from a vantage point of interest and curiosity as I wonder how I'll be different and what new experiences I can create in my life as a result of my efforts. Remember, work doesn't mean drudgery. It can be a source of great pleasure and satisfaction as you experience the fruits of your labor.

> *Life is a great big canvas,*
> *and you should throw all the paint*
> *on it you can.*
> *—Danny Kaye*

Chapter Three

Clear Those Rocks and Pull Those Weeds—
Recognize and Eliminate Negative Patterns

In any garden, uncontrolled weeds can choke out the flowers.
Negative patterns are the weeds of our minds: stealing nutrients and light,
competing for growing space, digging their roots deep into our identities,
sowing their seeds for future growth. Just as unchecked weeds take over a garden,
negative patterns will take over our lives unless we intentionally take steps to root
them out. Pulling the weeds of negativity can be hard work, but the results are well
worth the effort: a life that is lush, fruitful and growing.

You know you have a negative pattern working in your life when the same frustrating events happen over and over again; when you still feel angry, sad or afraid because of something that occurred in your life; when you feel like you overreact easily and often. If you are not enjoying your life, if you are not experiencing success and well-being, chances are there is a negative pattern at work. All of us have some negative patterning. This patterning becomes a problem when it prevents us from creating the lives we want or enjoying the lives we have. In this chapter, I'll give you the tools you need to overcome problematic negative patterns. Here are the four negative patterns we'll be working on:

- *Limiting beliefs.* A negative perception that you believe to be true and accurate about yourself, others or the world.

- *Past events.* Past incidents that continue to affect how you understand and interpret current situations.

- *Schemas.* An operating system, or mind-program, which affects how your brain filters and processes information it receives.

- *Emotional hijacks.* Overwhelming negative emotions that prevent you from thinking clearly or reacting objectively to events and situations.

These four negative patterns interact with each other and can impact your growth. Like an acorn growing into an oak, each of us has an innate potential. Just as rocks and pollutants can stunt the oak's growth, our negative patterns can block us from realizing our full capabilities. *Limiting beliefs* are like the rocks that prevent the tree from sinking its roots down as far as it would like; they block our ability to achieve our true potential. *Past events* are like toxic poisons that infect the soil; they pollute our thinking and our belief systems. *Schemas* act like pollution and other environmental filters that prevent healthy sunlight and rain from nourishing the tree; they prevent beneficial beliefs from occurring to us and set up a system for negative self-fulfilling prophecies. *Emotional hijacks* are like kudzu, vines that grow so extensively they can destroy a tree; they act like weeds, cutting off the thinking part of our brains and keeping us stuck in negative and emotional reactions. If a tree has to expend all of its energy in dealing with environmental stressors like rocks or drought, it can't grow well and become healthy. Like the tree, if all of *your* energy is diverted to fighting destructive patterns, like obsessing about your past or filtering everything through negative schemas, you won't be as strong and healthy as possible either.

Our goal here is to get rid of negative patterns so that you can reach your own potential and become your best self. You have to recognize when a pattern is affecting you. This is step one. You can't just identify the negative pattern and expect it to go away. You have to create alternatives so that you can effectively replace the old pattern with a new one. This is the second step.

Step One: Recognize when a pattern is affecting you
Step Two: Replace these patterns with healthy, new alternatives

Here's something to keep in mind when you're working through this process. When you're replacing an old habit with a new one, there will be some time when *both exist at the same time*. So, let's go back to one of my limiting beliefs: I'm too heavy to be attractive and loved. I want to replace this belief with a more realistic belief, that I'm actually pretty and sexy. In doing so, there was a time when *both* thoughts co-existed and I felt fat *and* sexy at the same time, and I experienced myself as both at the same time. Only by going through the process of feeling both beliefs can you create the healthier pathway and the new vision of yourself. You can be the new without having successfully banished the old completely. Keep this in mind because when you feel the pull of the old thoughts, you can make the mistake of thinking you've failed in your efforts to create a new pattern, and you may give up. What you have to do, really, is to allow yourself to have both thoughts because you're reinforcing the new and healthy pathway and eventually it will replace the old pathway. That said, let's look at each of these negative patterns more closely.

LIMITING BELIEFS

Remember that a *limiting belief* is a negative perception that you believe to be true and accurate about yourself, others or the world. Have you ever woken up in the morning and been cheerful and happy and then said to yourself, "Oh, wait, this is my life," and suddenly you're not in a cheerful mood anymore? You have just remembered all of your limiting beliefs, and they ruined your good mood. This is what I call "picking up the rock."

Rocks represent limiting beliefs that we think are true and that weigh us down. We can pick them up without being aware of it because our rocks are so familiar, so comforting and so much a part of us. Now, imagine that we're all swimming through the "Lake of Life." As we swim, we are only using one arm because we are holding our rock with the other. There are people on the shore who can see that we're having trouble swimming, and they know we'd be a lot better off if we weren't trying to get along with only one arm. They're shouting at us: *"Drop the rock!"* The thing is, we are so attached to our rocks that we can't see or hear the people on the shore who are giving us important information that contradicts our limiting beliefs. Our negative perceptions are so strong we would rather end up drowning than let go of that rock. It's time to start listening to those people on the shore, and drop those rocks!

Ridding Your Garden of the Rocks of Limiting Beliefs

There are four steps to overcoming limiting beliefs: recognize the limiting belief; reexamine the limiting belief; react against the limiting belief and re-create the limiting belief into an empowering belief.

Overcoming a Limiting Belief

- Recognize
- Reexamine
- React
- Re-create

Recognize the Rocks in Your Garden. The first step in getting rid of limiting beliefs is being able to identify them. You have to recognize that you are, in fact, carrying a rock or a limiting belief before you can put it down. Now, how can you tell if you're carrying around a rock? If you have a belief that prevents you from creating conditions for success and promoting a sense of well-being, this is a limiting belief. It restricts your thinking, constricts your energy and hinders your vision.

Here's an example of one of my limiting beliefs. Before I was a therapist, I was a teacher. My limiting belief when I was a teacher was that I was terrible. I said to myself, "Oh, these poor students. All the other teachers are better than I am. It's so sad that they got stuck with me as their teacher." Then I became a therapist and my limiting belief was (you can probably guess) the same. I'd think, "Oh, my poor clients. All the other therapists are better than I am. I'm embarrassed to take money for this. They should probably go see someone else who can help them more." Very heavy, this rock.

I would become so upset about my performance (either as a teacher or a therapist) that I literally felt like I was drowning. In this emotional state, I was unable to create conditions for success because I couldn't recognize my strengths and assets. I suffered a great deal, but not once did this limiting belief help me improve my performance. I certainly wasn't promoting a sense of well-being and security.

Reexamine the Limiting Belief. The first step is to recognize and identify your limiting beliefs. The second step is to let go of the limiting belief—to stop believing in the rock. It can be really hard to do this for ourselves, because our commitment to the limiting belief can be very strong. Often, you have to listen to the people who are on the shore of your Lake of Life who are giving you feedback. They're the ones saying that this is a rock, a problem, a limiting belief about yourself.

I had a limiting belief that I wasn't a good teacher. Even though I got lots of positive evaluations from my students, I would look through the pile of positive evaluations until I found an evaluation that was even slightly negative, and then I'd say, "Oh my god! I knew it! I'm a bad teacher!" Because of my limiting belief, I didn't *see* the ones that were positive, and I certainly didn't give them any credence. I call this "negative shopping," the unconscious compulsion to look for the bad in any given situation.

By engaging in negative shopping, I was totally ignoring the people who gave me positive evaluations who were standing on the shore saying *"Drop the rock."* The fact is, you can never get a 100 percent positive response on anything. I'm not going to get every single person in a class or a training to say that I'm the best teacher ever. That's not reality ... but neither is it realistic to walk around only listening to the negatives in life, which is what I had been doing.

React Against the Limiting Belief. Try to understand where your rocks come from. This can help change your perspective by uncovering hidden factors that produced the limiting belief and intensified its importance. As you begin to understand the root causes of your belief, you can release and resolve feelings and begin to experience the belief as something separate from who you really are. In other words, your limiting belief no longer remains attached to your "true self." A lot of rocks come from childhood, from the culture, from the media. They come from our peers. Some of my biggest rocks came from feeling unpopular and unattractive in high school. By understanding the origin of the limiting beliefs, you give yourself ammunition to let them go. You begin to realize that the origin of the belief is no longer relevant in your current life, and in fact, may never have been valid.

That's not to say that you have to know exactly where your rocks came from. First, you may not be able to trace the origin of the rock. Second, we can pick up rocks so unconsciously that we don't even remember where they came from. Third, while I think it's important to understand our past and be aware of it, this knowledge won't help you get rid of your problems. I can tell you ten reasons that may explain why I feel insecure about my professional abilities, but the fact that I can understand it intellectually doesn't mean I will change my belief. Only by reacting against the limiting belief will it lose its persuasive appeal. You need to literally say, "I no longer choose to believe this about myself, others or life."

Re-create Your Limiting Belief into an Empowering Belief. The next step is to re-create the limiting belief so that it creates *conditions for success and promotes a sense of well-being.* What would that be for me, in terms of my self-conception as a teacher or trainer? What I now say to myself is: "I am a good therapist, and I'm getting better with experience." This is true. This statement recognizes that I'm good at what I do, and also nods to the fact that I'm always evolving. There are two techniques that can help you create a correct connection and turn your limiting belief into an empowering belief.

First, you can use a *"counter belief."* Take the limiting belief and shift it from something negative to something positive. In terms of my teaching, instead of saying to myself, "I'm a bad teacher," I'll instead repeat the counter belief, which is the opposite statement: a statement that is 180 degrees opposite to the limiting belief. Mine would be, "I'm a good teacher." This is my empowering belief. What's yours? Repeat this as often as necessary until you can start to chip away at the limiting belief and reduce its hold on you.

Sometimes it doesn't feel like you can believe the opposite of the limiting belief. You are not yet ready to let it go, or it feels like too far of a stretch. If this is the case for you, use the *"inclusion technique."* With this strategy, you keep the limiting belief while adding a counter belief. So, I might say to myself, "I'm not the perfect teacher, *and* I'm becoming better at it." Be sure to use *and* when joining the two statements. We have a tendency to say "but," which minimizes the new counter statement. Joining the new counter statement to the limiting belief helps to create a bridge to truly feeling the reality of the counter statement. Here's another example: "I am not as good as I want to be, *and* I am learning and gaining experience." The inclusion technique allows you to shift your focus while minimizing discomfort. Both strategies lift and expand you instead of pulling you into a downward spiral.

We are what we think. All that we are arises with our thoughts.
With our thoughts, we make our world. —Buddha

Here is a list of common limiting beliefs.[1] Which ones pertain to you? Don't worry if you have a lot of check marks on this list. Often, limiting beliefs are related to each other, so working on one belief is actually working on many at the same time. To practice "dropping your rock," choose one limiting belief that you connect with strongly. Now, reexamine that belief by finding evidence that disputes it. Next, make a commitment to react against it whenever it shows up in your life. Finally, re-create the limiting belief into an empowering belief using either the counter statement or inclusion techniques. Say the empowering belief out loud many times. Remember, repetition is key to creating new pathways. As you say your new belief, listen to the words and take them in as your new reality. You might notice that different limiting beliefs have more sway at certain times, so repeat this process whenever you notice a limiting belief blocking your path.

Limiting Beliefs List

❏ I'm not very smart.

❏ I'm not as good as the people I'm competing with.

❏ I never come out on top.

❏ No matter how good things start out, something always ruins my efforts.

❏ I cannot really change; I just am who I am.

❏ I don't have the family background to be what I really want to be.

❏ I've never been able to do it before. Why get my hopes up now?

❏ If I get too happy and relaxed, something will go wrong.

❏ If people really knew how much of the time I was "faking it," I would really be in trouble.

❏ If I tried to change, it would just upset other people.

❏ It's selfish of me to spend so much time and energy on me.

❏ I don't deserve a second chance.

❏ I don't really have the power to change my life.

❏ I don't know how to deal with difficult things.

❏ I'm not good enough.

❏ I don't have what it takes to be successful.

❏ I'm not worthy.

❏ Life is a struggle.

❏ Nothing I do makes a difference.

❏ Something bad always happens to me.

❏ I don't have the ability to sustain any changes.

❏ I'm a victim of forces beyond my control.

❏ I don't count.

❏ I need to always accommodate others or there will be problems.

❏ When someone is in trouble, I must always help them.

❏ It is shameful to make a mistake.

❏ I better not rock the boat or things could get worse.

❏ What I think or say won't make a difference.

❏ Nobody cares how I feel.

❏ Nobody cares what I think.

❏ I'm too old to learn new things.

❏ I will not be liked if I am too successful.

❏ I've got to do it myself if I am going to be successful.

❏ It's a dog-eat-dog world.

❏ _____ (other)

❏ _____ (other)

Rocks Get Pushed Up in the Soil

Have you ever noticed that, after it rains, rocks seem to spontaneously appear in the garden? The rain somehow forces rocks up and they pop out on top of the soil. The rocks in our emotional gardens are the same way; they can reappear even when we think they've all been removed. You will probably have to drop your own particular rock over and over again, because you will pick it up again without even noticing it.

Last summer, I was a mentor in a summer program for teenage girls and, even though I had dropped my limiting beliefs about my skills as a teacher and speaker, I managed to pick up my rock just for this activity. In the three days I participated in the program, I managed to convince myself that the girls I was mentoring would rather have had a different mentor. With all of my awareness, I *still* got triggered, and I picked up the rock again.

You need to continuously remain aware of how you're thinking about events, because the rock will just creep back into your garden if you're not careful! Fortunately, I was able to recognize that I had picked up my old rock, and I followed the steps described here. With effort, I was able to let go of this belief—again—and think more positively about myself. When rocks get pushed up through the soil, or are dropped in your garden by someone else, use the experience as an opportunity to continue growing and learning by clearing out the rocks again and observing what you learn in the process.

PAST EVENTS

Past events act as negative patterns when experiences in the present time are *filtered and interpreted* through the lens of the past and the memory of things that happened to you then. Past events that are unresolved and continue to carry a lot of emotion can overwhelm people with negative thoughts and feelings. The influence of past events can cause you to react in the present moment based on what happened to you in the past. Essentially, troublesome past events act like toxins, poisoning your current experiences. You can't be spontaneous and open to the possibilities of the present moment when you can't let go of the past.

We can all think of friends or relatives who are harboring a grudge or living in the past. For example, several years ago, a friend's husband left her for a younger woman. My friend is still really furious about the divorce and angry at her ex-husband. She spends huge amounts of emotional energy holding on to her feelings for a person who isn't even in her life anymore. In the process, she's making her life miserable.

Sometimes, people live in the past through negative self-perceptions. One of my clients is a man who had a hard time in elementary and middle school and was bullied and teased a lot. He retains that self-perception and still views himself through the eyes of his classmates, all of whom are decades older now. He spends enormous amounts of emotional energy holding onto a self-perception about himself that is years out of date.

A past event is, essentially, a memory. The first time the event happened, you interpreted it *as it happened* and formed a memory of it based on that interpretation. Memories are neither good nor bad. They can generate thoughts and feelings that take you on an upward spiral or a downward spiral, depending on how you have interpreted them. Our feelings about past events are created entirely by our thoughts and our interpretations about what happened, precisely because we are reacting to something that is over. Because the event is long gone, and your interpretation and thoughts about it determine how you feel about it, the role of that past event can be changed by changing your interpretation of it. I need to say that again because it's so important: *you can change the role of the past event in your life by changing the interpretations and thoughts that you bring to it.*

It's safe to say that if you're fixating on the past, you're spiraling *downward*. Focusing on something that can't be changed makes you a victim because it strengthens negativity rather than optimism. Your task is to change that spiral by looking at the past from a different perspective and finding a new interpretation. You can't go back and change what happened in the past. The only thing you can change about a past event is how you're going to interpret it and what you're going to learn from it, and that *is* possible. You can develop new interpretations of a past event that are based on who you are *at this point in time*, not who you were when the event originally happened. Reinterpreting the past gives you back control over your life. It allows you to choose an interpretation that enhances the present.

Have you ever gone back to your old elementary school or to the neighborhood where you grew up? When you think about those places, they probably seem really large in your mind. I always thought of my elementary school as having towering sliding boards and incredibly long hallways. My neighborhood seemed huge, and the corner store was really far away. Of course, that's just how I remembered it. Those were the interpretations and memories that I had formed. When I once went back, I was surprised to see that it was all different from the way I remembered! My school was tiny, the sliding boards were child-sized, and the hallways were totally normal. My old neighborhood turned out to be a compact place where everything was easily within walking distance. Now, nothing *shrank* since I was a kid. I'd just formed memories with my child's eyes, and I had attached meaning to them that was larger than my adult reality.

Past events are just like this. You can revisit them—like returning to your old school or neighborhood—the same way. You can go back to your memories of past events and see how they look today. This can help you reinterpret the events and make a better meaning for your current life. If you're having trouble creating conditions for success, think about whether you continue to carry around a past event that has a strong negative charge for you in the present moment. It can be hard to do this, but here are some questions to ask yourself:

- Are you still holding on to a personal label you got in the past?

- Is there a relationship from your past that continues to trouble you today?

- Do you have a negative job experience that stops you from moving forward in your career?

- Are there events from your life that produce considerable fear, sadness or anger when you think about them now?

- Are you resentful towards anyone or anything in your life?

- Do you have "unfinished business" that you avoid taking care of?

These questions can help you spot toxic past events so you can start letting them go.

Moving Beyond the Influence of Past Events

Once you have recognized a potent past event and identified the negative meanings associated with it, it's time to neutralize the past event through reinterpretation.[2] Here's how it works:

Letting Go of Past Events Through Reinterpretation

- Specify the event
- Identify the event's negative meaning for you
- Create a new interpretation of the event
- Let go of the event
- Take responsibility for your role

Specify the event. Recognize the event from your past that continues to have an emotional charge and that is preventing you from achieving success and well-being. Here's one of mine. When I was 15, my best friend told me that I would never get married unless I lost weight.

Identify the negative meaning. What are the thoughts, feelings and behaviors that come from the event? Examine the negative interpretations or meanings that you attached to the event. For me, I internalized my friend's message and made it mean that I was too fat for a boy or man to ever love me, and I wouldn't get married. I felt rejected, hurt and filled with self-loathing. I was afraid to talk to boys and to date. I hid my body by wearing baggy clothing.

Create a new interpretation of the event. Explore the event from a different perspective. Think about it from the vantage point of adulthood or through the eyes of another person. Find a meaning that will enable you to create an upward spiral in your current life. After all, you choose your interpretations, so create one that is empowering for you. In my case, I realized that my friend loved me and was trying to protect me from rejection. I also realized that she had internalized messages about society's expectations about girls' bodies, and her anxiety about my desire to date was also a reflection of her own fears about being attractive.

Let go of the incident. Forgive the person or people who hurt you, and let the incident go. I forgave my friend because she probably had no idea that I reacted so strongly to her comment. She wasn't trying to hurt my feelings.

Take responsibility for your role. Be aware of any continued negative charge you feel. It's important to understand and accept your own part in keeping the past alive. If you find that the past event continues to create a downward spiral, it is up to you to keep working on letting it go.

A Note About Forgiveness and Guilt

Let me talk a little bit about forgiveness, which many people find difficult to embrace. What I mean by forgiveness is *letting go of a hurt so you can move ahead.* Forgiveness is not about *forgetting* what happened to you, or *condoning* another person's bad behavior or necessarily *reconciling* with someone who hurt you. The purpose of forgiveness has nothing to do with the people who hurt you. They aren't even involved. It *is* all about you and your ability to move ahead. If someone has done something terrible to you, and you cannot forgive them, that person still has power over you. You will *stay* disempowered as long as you continue to focus on something that is past and that you can't change now. Forgiveness is a gift to yourself, and holding onto the past will stunt your growth. Think about the great leaders who have truly changed societies and improved life for people: Nelson Mandela, Mahatma Gandhi, the Dali Llama, Martin Luther King. All of these leaders incorporated forgiveness into their philosophies, recognizing that forgiveness is not only transformative, but also essential for growth.

> *The weak can never forgive.*
> *Forgiveness is the attribute of the strong.*
> —Gandhi.

People can be deeply invested in not letting go because it can feel like their hurt over the bad things *is* who they are. Letting go of anger or resentment might make a person feel unlike himself. It can feel very strange and unfamiliar, but over-identifying with the negative obscures the *true essence* of who you are. The negative past does not define you. It is just hiding the true self, the free self, the self that is not bitter. Continuing to hold onto anger, resentment and bitterness prevents growth. Forgiving others and letting go allows yourself to be free to create success and well-being in your present and your future.

The same is true about guilt, which can also overwhelm a person and keep her trapped in the past. Guilt is your mind's way of alerting you that you've strayed off course from your true self. Guilt is saying "that wasn't appropriate; that's not who you are." The healthy response is not to beat yourself up about whatever is making you feel guilty, but to take note of it and change your behavior next time. It's important to remember that *I made a mistake* isn't the same thing as *I am a mistake.* Everyone makes mistakes; it's entirely human. You are *not* the mistake you made. You feel the guilt so you can learn from it and do something different the next time you are in a similar situation.

Toxic guilt is guilt that you can't let go of. It's what you experience when you continually think and obsess about an event and beat yourself up about what happened. Wallowing in toxic guilt doesn't do anything to help you learn, grow or change. It keeps you from honoring your own feelings and listening to your internal feedback. In this way, toxic guilt keeps itself alive and keeps you mired in negativity.

When we're talking about forgiving people and letting go of the bad things that others have done to you, one very important person to add to the list is yourself. In fact, you should be at the *top* of the list. Letting go, moving forward and putting your energy into healthy things all apply to yourself as well as to others who may have hurt you before. Remember to be as nice to yourself as you want to be to others.

It is possible to recognize the need to let go of the past and to forgive yourself and others but difficult to do so on an emotional level. Here are several ideas that can help you.

- *Practice Neutrality*: Every time you feel a negative charge from a past event, treat it as if it were a cloud passing on the horizon. Acknowledge it, and then dismiss it from your mind. Continue doing this until you can feel neutral about the memory of the past event.

- *Keep a journal*: As you write about the event, let your feelings fill the page spontaneously. Don't judge or edit yourself. When you've run out of steam, ask yourself, "Am I ready to let this go?" If the answer is no, keep writing and exploring. The issue doesn't have to be resolved at this moment in time. If the answer is yes, write a commitment to yourself to let it go. You may have to repeat this process several times. Letting go is like peeling an onion; sometimes many layers have to come off before you're done.

- *Write a letter*: Not a letter you would actually mail, this is just a way to communicate your feelings. Write a letter telling the other person (or people) involved in the event how you feel, and how the event impacted you. Next, tell them your new interpretation of the event; describe how you have forgiven them and moved on with your life. End the letter by telling them what you appreciate about yourself. You can write to yourself, too.

- *Work with symbols:* Make an object that represents the event. Symbolically let go of the object by actually releasing the representation. You can bury the object, burn it, place it in a stream, throw it in the air or drop it in the trash. You may also wish to transform it into a new object, to symbolize the learning you've gotten from processing the past event.

- *Learn more about forgiveness:* There are many books and resources with explanations and exercises about the forgiveness process. They can help you to learn more about it and work on your issues more deeply. Some suggestions are listed in the last chapter.

- *Seek professional help:* It may be that you want help in working on these issues. Therapy is very useful in providing the skills and encouragement needed to let go of harmful past events and forgive oneself and others.

SCHEMAS

Schemas are mind-programs that process information and create expectations.[3] Your computer needs an operating system in order for the programs to run. Your brain is the same way. A schema is just like an operating system for the brain. Schemas influence how we perceive, remember and evaluate information about ourselves, other people and life events. Schemas become *self-fulfilling* models of your world. Because schemas are the filters through which you see the world, the world bends to fit the schema. Your brain selects information that fits the schema and filters out all other data. It is this process of "selective perception" that makes faulty schemas so powerful.

Below is a list of common maladaptive schemas that show up in people's personal and work lives. Take a look at this list and see which schemas seem familiar. I've added questions to help you identify your schemas. What issues keep showing up in your life? Do you constantly feel like you're abandoned in your relationships? You probably have an "abandonment schema." Do you feel exhausted from doing things for other people? You probably have a "subjugation schema." Some schemas are related, so you may notice you have a cluster of schemas that reinforce each other.

Ten Schemas that Pollute Your Life

1. Abandonment. The perception that people you love are unavailable for support and connection.

- Are you sensitive to rejection?
- Are you afraid people will leave you?
- Do you need repeated reassurances to feel secure?

2. Mistrust and Abuse: The expectation that others will hurt, humiliate, manipulate or take advantage of you.

- Do you believe other people are taking advantage of you or have hidden motives, even without concrete proof?
- Are you hesitant to share personal information for fear others will use it against you?
- Do you give in to others because you are afraid of them and/or their reaction?

3. Dependence: The belief that you are unable to handle everyday responsibilities in a competent manner without the help of others.

- Do you have difficulty making decisions?

- Do you avoid new challenges on your own?
- Are you unsure about areas of practical functioning and daily survival?

4. *Vulnerability*: The exaggerated fear that disaster, such as natural, criminal, medical or financial catastrophes, could strike at any time.

- Are you constantly worried that something bad is about to happen to you?
- Are you anxious about terrible things happening to people close to you?
- Do you feel you lack the ability to cope with the possible dangers of life?

5. *Emotional Deprivation*: The expectation that your need for love will not be adequately met by others.

- Do you feel like other people often don't come through for you?
- Do you believe other people don't understand how you feel?
- Do you think other people don't care enough about you?

6. *Social Exclusion*: The feeling that you are different from other people and not part of any group or community.

- Do you feel inferior to the people around you?
- Are you nervous and self-conscious in groups of people?
- Do you avoid joining groups and keep to yourself?

7. *Defectiveness*: The feeling that you are bad, unwanted, unlovable, inferior or invalid in important respects.

- Do you hide parts of your true self from others?
- Do you put yourself down around others?
- Do you feel anxious even when you are successful because you worry that you can't maintain your success?

8. *Failure*: The belief that you are fundamentally inadequate, relative to your peers, in areas of achievement (such as school, career, sports) and that you will, therefore, inevitably fail.

- Did you choose a career below your potential?
- Do you avoid taking steps to develop your skills?
- Do you feel like an imposter even when you are objectively successful?

9. *Subjugation*: The belief that it is necessary to sacrifice your needs and desires to please other people.

- Do you usually let other people have their own way?
- Do you avoid confrontation?
- Is it hard for you to do or say something that might hurt another person's feelings?

10. *Unrelenting Standards*: The need to meet high, internalized standards of behavior and performance in order to avoid criticism; perfectionism.

- Does your whole life seem to revolve around success?
- Does your health suffer because of self-imposed stress?
- Do you feel overwhelmed because you are trying to accomplish so much?

How do schemas show up in your life? I'd like to share a significant illustration from my life. I was 40 years old, single and looking to be in a long-term relationship leading to marriage. At a professional workshop, I was introduced to the concept of schemas and decided to understand how they were operating in my life. I learned that I had abandonment and emotional deprivation schemas, and upon examining my relationship history with men, I had a "major aha!" I realized that I was being drawn to men who were interested in other women in addition to me or who were disinterested in moving towards commitment. I was a victim to the schemas' filtering systems, selecting men who would invariably leave me, be unavailable for support and unable to love me. The repetition of this pattern in my relationships with men stunned me and jolted me into a new awareness of my role in creating this self-fulfilling prophesy.

Here is another story about two friends of mine who were dealing with defective and failure schemas. Diane and Rachel both serve on the board of directors of a social service agency. Diane had just ended her term as president of the board and turned over the role to Rachel. Diane received appreciation from the board for her work as president but secretly felt inadequate and as if she were an imposter. Rachel was feeling anxious and worried about her ability to succeed in this new role.

Their schemas became evident during a conversation they had about James, a long-term board member who was now eager to become more active in the organization. Diane had always thought James was capable and smart and regretted that he hadn't given much time to the organization during her tenure. She assumed his lack of involvement was because of her, and blurted out to Rachel, "I guess he didn't like working with me, so he waited until I wasn't president anymore to get more involved!" Rachel started laughing, and said, "And here I thought James wanted to be more involved now because he didn't trust me to be a good president, and wanted to keep track of what I was doing!" The truth was, James had just recently freed up time from his work duties so he could devote more energy to the board. Both Diane and Rachel later realized that they repeatedly misinterpret situations because of mind-programs based on feelings of defectiveness and failure.

People often say to me, "What if I really *were* abandoned?" "What if I really am a failure?" They fear that their schemas are concrete and unchangeable. Nothing is set in stone. The world isn't black and white. No one has been abandoned by *everyone* they know. No one is a failure at *everything*. You have to be able to gather appropriate information about your life and find an area where the schema is weak. A common error people make is to try to replace a powerful schema with its opposite, which doesn't work. If your schema is that you are unlovable, you can't try to make yourself believe that "everyone loves me." That would be delusional. In the same way, an abandonment schema can't be flipped on its head from "everyone will leave me" to "everyone will always be there for me." Instead, an adaptive schema would be to say, "I am loved by so-and-so," or "People will be as supportive as they can." If you think of the schema as a coin, the goal is not to just flip the coin over to its other side. You want to *change* the coin totally. Our goal is to replace your schema with one that is positive, one that helps you spiral upward and achieve success. This requires discipline and practice to accomplish.

> The only limits to our realization of tomorrow
> will be our doubts of today.   —Franklin D. Roosevelt

Cultivating Beneficial Schemas

Take some time to look over the list of faulty schemas. Think about which ones might be affecting your life. Here are the steps to replace ineffective schemas with productive ones:

Replacing Faulty Schemas

- Understand the origins and triggers of your schema
- Build a case against your schema
- Develop new, productive mind-programs
- Experience new thoughts, feelings and behaviors
- Keep practicing

Understand the origins and triggers of your schema. First, examine experiences from your family, school, peers and friends, religious and cultural background. Use this information to separate the schema from your authentic self. Recognize how and why you developed this mind-program. Sometimes we are unaware of the origins of our ineffective schemas because we developed them unconsciously. Even if you don't know why you developed a particular schema, you can still choose to let it go.

Next, become aware of the schema's pull. This is the first step in ending its power. Discover your triggers—people or situations that set off your schema. When your schema is operating, ask yourself:

- What do I think?
- How do I feel?
- What do I do?

Build a case against your schema. Ineffective schemas continue to influence our perceptions because we don't stop to objectively examine them. We just assume the information they filter is accurate. Try to step outside your schema to get a clear view of the evidence. List the evidence from your current life that supports your schema. Then, list the evidence that *contradicts* your schema. Review the lists and ask yourself:

- Does any evidence indicate the schema is inherently true of me?
- If the schema (or some part of the schema) seems true, what can I do to change this aspect of myself?

The goal is to recognize the way faulty schemas operate in your life so you can intervene to change them.

Develop new, productive mind-programs. In order to break the strength of the old schema, you must actively and intentionally develop new schemas. Remember, effective mind-programs are balanced, flexible, realistic and empowering. Here are examples of beneficial schemas that replace the ineffective ones presented earlier. Use these as a guide to develop adaptive mind-programs that fit the way you want to be.

1. *Intimate:* I choose people who are stable and committed, and I am comfortable with normal separations.

2. *Trusting:* I generally trust people unless they give me reason not to. I prevent others from taking advantage of me.

3. *Capable:* I am capable of handling everyday decisions and responsibilities. I ask for help when I need it.

4. *Hardy:* I can bounce back if bad things happen.

5. *Worthy:* I deserve to have my needs met, but not at another's expense. I feel I am as good as other people.

6. *Social acceptance:* I make a concerted effort to be myself. I give myself a chance to connect to others.

7. *Desirable*: I am comfortable with my looks, social skills and other characteristics.

8. *Adequate*: I appreciate my success, and at the same time, I feel good about myself regardless of my accomplishments.

9. *Assertive*: My needs and desires are important, and I express them to others.

10. *Reasonable Expectations*: I enjoy myself and my life as I give up perfections and focus on balance.

Experience new thoughts, feelings and behaviors. Imagine yourself in a situation that would trigger the schema you are working to replace. Now think of a person, either real or fictional, who can be a role model for your new mind-program. This person functions like an emotional coach to help you respond using your new mind-program. Think about how your role model might react to the trigger, and ask yourself:

- What new thoughts would I have?
- What new feelings would I have?
- What new actions would I take?

Strive to integrate these thoughts, feelings and actions into your experience.

Keep Practicing! Schemas want to stay in place because they think they are us, and they want to live through us. Schemas started for a reason, and they believe that we need them. Tell your schema it is being "upgraded" to a new and improved "operating system."

EMOTIONAL HIJACKS

An emotional hijack occurs when you are taken over by a sudden, intense and irrational negative feeling. Did you ever have the experience of "going off" after someone pushed a "hot button," only to look back and realize you totally overreacted? This is an emotional hijack. We are often hijacked by our limiting beliefs, unresolved past events and schemas, but hijacks occur for lots of reasons. My most memorable hijack was the time I got into a fight with a co-worker. We were in a power struggle over division of duties. One day, he left a pile of folders on my desk. I entered my office in a calm mood, but after seeing those folders, I was throwing them across his desk within seconds and screaming something I no longer remember. I escaped into the stairwell to dissolve into tears. I knew I had been hijacked because when I looked back on the event, I realized the amount and intensity of my emotional reaction was inappropriate to the situation. Not only that, it hindered a resolution and destroyed my reputation in the department.

Emotional hijacks are created by the same part of the brain that produces the "fight or flight" impulse, an area called the *amygdala*.[4] When something threatens someone, the brain bypasses the conscious mind and sends the signal straight to this ancient part of the brain, where it sets off an early warning system. This process happens automatically and is extremely fast. When the brain gets the message about the danger, it floods the body with adrenaline and stress hormones that make us want to react *instantly*. Our heart rate and breathing speed up, our digestion stops and the brain sends blood to our muscles in case we need to make a quick get-away. Our bodies are primed for action—to respond to the danger either by fighting or fleeing from it.

The amygdala response is hard-wired into the brain and, over the vast amount of time that humans have been on earth, it's served us well. Evolutionarily, this impulse has protected us in times of danger, when our earliest ancestors were menaced by ravenous predators and fighting for survival. Sometimes today, there is a specific danger we need to react to, such as an impending car accident or a potential mugging, but more often than not, the amygdala now responds to emotional stresses, such as the one I just described with my co-worker.

An emotional hijack feels so overwhelming and uncontrollable because it is set off by our amygdala, which resides in the oldest, most primitive part of our brain. Our logical, thinking brain is out of the loop. Because the amygdala is designed to respond within nanoseconds, it bases an emotional reaction on generalizations and broad-based assumptions. This means we get emotionally flooded even when there is no real danger. You may have had this same experience from something relatively simple like giving a public speech. There isn't any real danger but the emotional hijack feels just as powerful as when our ancestors were staring down the wolves.

Emotional hijacks can affect how we act and feel in both personal and professional environments, and they can seriously affect a person's ability to succeed. For example, a study of store managers at a large American retail chain found that those managers who were the least able to handle their emotions were tense, beleaguered and overwhelmed by pressures. Further, these managers ran stores with the *worst* performance in the chain, as measured by net profits, sales per square foot, sales per employee and sales for every dollar of inventory investment. Managers who stayed the most composed under the same pressures of running their stores were the managers who handled their emotional hijacks the best, and they had the *best* sales records in the chain.

While the common term is "fight or flight," people's individual responses to emotional hijacks are actually a bit more complicated. Based on our own personalities and life histories, an emotional hijack may cause us to want to *fight,* in which case the emotional response is experienced as anger, or to *flee,* a desire to run away or withdraw. It may also lead us to *freeze,* becoming immobilized and seemingly unable to make any response; to feel *faint,* in which case we experience confusion or numbness; or to *fret,* responding to the danger by obsessively ruminating and worrying about it.

Reactions to Hijacks:

- Fight
- Flee
- Freeze
- Faint
- Fret

Weeding Out Emotional Hijacks

The goal is to learn to prevent emotional hijacks by retraining the brain's response to danger. You will probably not be able to eliminate emotional hijacks *entirely,* but you can retrain your brain (your amygdala) to respond differently when it perceives something that it interprets as dangerous. If you think back to the earlier discussion of the way the brain works, you'll recall that a default pathway is a habit that the brain gets into and a pattern of behavior that it falls back upon. When the amygdala is triggered and you experience an emotional hijack, the brain automatically moves to its defensive default pathway. The pathways can be set up by your childhood experiences, your family, your life experiences or messages that we receive from society, the media, religious institutions or other cultural entities. All of these things contribute to the formation of brain patterns. As you retrain your brain to develop new pathways, your emotional hijacks will become less frequent, less intense and last for less time. The approaches to managing emotional hijacks are each designed to help you retrain your brain.

Managing Emotional Hijacks

- Practice self-observation
- Recognize the first signs of a hijack
- Delay your reaction and examine your experience
- Change your automatic thoughts
- Separate feelings from reality
- Do or say something different

Practice self-observation. By paying attention to your own moods and reactions, you can identify when you've been emotionally hijacked and start to intervene with the thinking part of your brain. First, work on identifying what your triggers are, so that when a similar trigger happens in the future you will be able to understand what's really happening. Self-observation also includes reflecting back after a hijack and identifying what triggered it. It's also useful to keep track of how you respond when you're emotionally flooded. Do you start yelling? Do you withdraw quickly from conflict? All of this information will be helpful as you work to stop yourself from experiencing uncontrolled emotional hijacks.

Recognize the first signs of a hijack. Once you start to learn what your triggers are, you can begin to recognize when your thoughts are false and distorted. You can prepare yourself for the possible onset of a hijack. Remember, hijacks are automatic. While you can't necessarily prevent one, you can contain it. By intervening early, you can stop yourself from being swept away by emotional flooding. Check in with yourself and ask, "What are my bodily sensations that tell me a hijack is on the way?" You may feel nauseated, your heart may pound or you may feel flushed with heat or cold. Your throat may get tight, you may want to cry or you may lash out in anger. When you have these feelings in the future, you will know you are on the verge of being hijacked. Just recognizing that a hijack is upon you is enough to engage the thinking part of your brain. Once this happens, the emotional flooding can subside.

My friend, Nichole, used to get into a lot of fights with her boyfriend, Paul. Eventually, they realized that many of the arguments were precipitated by Nichole's fear of being abandoned and Paul's fear of being manipulated. When they fought, Paul and Nichole were "pushing each other's buttons," then getting emotionally hijacked and lashing out at the other person. Of course, once they were hijacked, they were too mad to really resolve anything, and their fights went round and round pointlessly. Now, when one person seems to be experiencing an emotional hijack, the other makes a buzzing noise, like a ringer being pushed: *bzzzz!* This is their shorthand for "Hey, I seem to have pushed a button; you're getting hijacked!" Having figured out what caused their emotional hijacks, Paul and Nichole are able to step back and settle their disagreements without so much drama.

Delay your reaction and examine your experience. Our brains automatically respond to emotional hijacks, and we are programmed to revert to the knee-jerk reactions I talked about earlier—to fight, freeze, faint, fret or flee. Instead of doing one of these the next time you're emotionally hijacked, see if you can sit with the body's response and the brain's thoughts. Examine the feeling you're having while knowing that you don't have to do anything about it. One particularly helpful strategy is to engage in the practice of "mindfulness." This is simply the practice of being aware of every moment and fully experiencing it. It means not judging or thinking, just observing what is happening. With this kind of detachment, you are likely to find that the normal slights and irritations of everyday life are really not that important, and you can learn to avoid an emotional reaction to them. Emotions, left alone, will dissipate on their own; if you continue to feed them through obsession or rumination, however, the emotions will gain strength.

One of my clients, Leo, used to get emotionally hijacked at work when his boss didn't praise his work on projects or acknowledge his contribution to the team efforts. Leo would often become upset and interpret her silence to mean that he hadn't been performing well enough to earn any praise or recognition. Afterwards, he sought out his boss in order to get reassurance about his performance from her, but Leo eventually recognized that she was growing impatient with this constant need for what she called "hand holding." Leo's boss was tired of telling him that she was satisfied with his work and thought he was a good team member (except for his constant need for reassurance). So, Leo decided to work on his reaction to the feelings of not getting enough praise. He would still get hijacked at times when he felt that his boss was not praising him enough. Despite this, he learned not to react to these feelings but instead to just sit with them. Leo acknowledged his inner experience, in which he felt devalued and inadequate, but recognized that the feeling did not reflect reality. In fact, he reminded himself that his boss had reassured him about his value countless times. Leo adopted a new operating principle that said, "My boss will tell me if there is a problem. If she doesn't say anything, it means everything is fine." With this internal message, his negative emotional reactions became weaker.

Change your automatic thoughts. This concept goes back to the idea of rewiring the brain to adopt healthy patterns in place of patterns that aren't working for you. Remember that you can consciously restructure the way your brain patterns work by changing your interpretations of events. Because people who are emotionally flooded are experiencing negative emotions such as fear or anger, their thoughts are also negative. Notice the automatic thoughts that occur when you are emotionally triggered; these are likely to be thoughts based on your limiting beliefs, past events or schemas. If you can intervene by changing how you are thinking about what's happening, you can begin to contain the flooding and quiet down the emotional hijack. The key is to come up with a new interpretation of the event that does not lead to negative emotions but instead puts you on an upward spiral.

Once, colleagues and I were eating lunch in the company cafeteria, and we made a spontaneous plan to get together and go dancing that Saturday night. Later that afternoon, I got a call from another friend, Janice. She had been in the cafeteria also, and overheard us making plans. She called because she was upset that she had been excluded from the outing since we hadn't invited her. She wanted to know if people had a problem with her or didn't like being around her. In fact, we hadn't thought about it, but might have assumed that she would be spending the evening with her husband. The group was perfectly happy to invite Janice to come out with us. Her automatic assumption, though, had been that we intentionally excluded her because she wasn't popular. Because of this assumption, she got quite upset and felt badly about herself. Thank goodness she called me to check out her feelings, or she might have retained those negative and inaccurate feelings which wouldn't have been good for her or our friendship. Another strategy for Janice might have been to reason with herself about how likely her automatic thoughts and fears were, or she could have thought of other possible explanations that weren't predicated on her insecurities.

Separate feeling from reality. An emotional hijack occurs with very basic feelings of anger, fear and sadness. The emotions that occur during an emotional hijack are very broad. They aren't subtle or nuanced in the way that happens when we can engage our logic or reason. This broad, negative feeling is not reality. You may be feeling like you're being abandoned, rejected or attacked, but that is only a constructed reality based on inaccurate feelings, memories and information. If you say to yourself, "This is just a feeling. It is not reality," it can help diffuse the power of the emotional hijack. Separating feelings from reality means recognizing that you don't have to make any actions or draw any conclusions from the feeling you're having. You don't have to use it as the basis of forming connections about the present experience.

My friend, Kate, loves to eat dry cereal late at night because it's crunchy and satisfying, and it gives her a nice serotonin boost that helps her sleep. She is very conscious of her weight, however, and her family always bugged her about being heavy when she was growing up. One day, Kate wanted some cereal after dinner and couldn't find any when she went into the pantry. She complained about this to her roommate, who said, "Yeah, you've really been eating a lot of it this week." Kate became really defensive and angry, and snapped at her roommate. In fact, the roommate's comment had been entirely neutral. Kate just responded to it with all the emotional negativity from her childhood, when her parents criticized her eating habits. By the next morning, Kate was able to see that her roommate's comments were just a statement of fact, not a personal indictment. She apologized for flying off the handle and resolved to think about where her emotional hijack might be coming from the next time she experienced one.

Do or say something different. Break the pattern of the negative emotion by reacting in a new way. This will help your brain to develop new pathways and weaken the pathway that triggers an emotional hijack. If you usually withdraw when you're emotionally hijacked, do something connective. Instead of walking away from someone you're fighting with, reach out a hand to them. If you usually shout and scream when you're mad, be quiet for once and see how that feels. Trying a new response will help your brain to learn creative and innovative responses to your traditional emotional triggers.

When my husband and I experience tension, my fall-back behavior is to flee to the bedroom. When I do this, I want him to come in and reach out to me, which is a reaction based on old schemas (abandonment and emotional deprivation) and old, habitual automatic behaviors. Instead of doing this (even though I still want to), I make myself leave the bedroom, go find him and give him a hug. Changing my behavior helps my brain let go of ingrained ways of responding and allows me to get past my emotional hijack more quickly.

When you get to the end of your rope—
tie a knot on it and hang on. —*Eleanor Roosevelt*

WEEDING IS A DAILY PROCESS

As anyone who has ever worked a garden knows, weeds are tenacious. They come back, and they are stubborn. As you pull out the weeds in your emotional garden, you may notice the same thing: your negative patterns are likely to be tenacious and stubborn, just like weeds. In fact, the old patterns tend to resurface as you make progress, especially in moments of stress, anxiety or vulnerability. For this reason, you will need to keep practicing the strategies to release negative patterns and continue to think about these issues on a regular basis.

It's helpful to keep in mind that change is a process. In working with any negative pattern, it's not possible to simply change it like you would turn off a light bulb. Personal change can't be controlled like an on-off switch; it truly is a *process*. Being aware of three key watchwords—frequency, intensity and duration—can help you stay focused on the process of change and not give up on it. Look for changes in *frequency* (how often the negative pattern comes up), *intensity* (how strong the pattern is), and *duration* (how long the feeling associated with the negative feeling lasts). Over time, all three should diminish: the negative pattern will come up less often, it will feel less intense and it will last for a shorter period of time. Checking out the three watchwords is a really helpful way of assessing how powerful your negative patterns are, and will help you observe and appreciate your progress as they weaken.

As I said earlier, some people will decide that they need help in doing this work. If that's the case for you, you will want to get professional assistance. Therapy can be immensely helpful in working on releasing negative patterns. The exercises and discussions in this chapter can help you decide if you want to do this on your own or if you would rather work with a professional by going into therapy. There's no right or wrong way to go about it. You have to decide what will work best for you.

Nobody can make you feel inferior without your consent.
—*Eleanor Roosevelt*

THE SOIL IS READY FOR PLANTING

Now that you've prepared the soil by clearing the rocks and pulling the weeds of your negative patterns, it's time to plant the seeds of optimism. To have a beautiful garden requires actively planting flowers. In the same way, cultivating optimism means integrating the five Practices of POWER Optimism into your day-to-day life.

The Seeds of POWER Optimism

Proactive—What can I do?

Open-minded—What are innovative responses?

Well-informed—What do I need to know?

Evolving—What can I learn?

Resilient—What is a motivating interpretation?

In the next section, we'll explore how to use these practices to create conditions for success and promote a sense of well-being. Each practice is paired with a question that helps you focus on the meaning behind the practice. Asking yourself these questions on a regular basis is a great way to put yourself on an upward spiral. In addition, you will learn three strategies for each practice. Using these strategies ensures that you are creating growth spurts—not growth slumps—in your life. At the end of each strategy, you will find a chart that summarizes the ideas and illustrates the difference between actions that lead to an upward spiral and those that result in a downward spiral.

As you start planting the seeds of POWER Optimism in your life, you will probably notice a desire to move forward as well as a fear of doing so. Both of these feelings can exist at the same time. It is important to begin to recognize for yourself when the fear you feel is legitimate or when it is the result of normal anxiety and excitement about change. One way to differentiate the two is to check in with yourself to see if the change is producing an upward or a downward spiral. Let me give you an example.

Before I started in private practice, I was working in a job that I had come to dislike because of one particular area of responsibility that I dreaded. I negotiated with my boss to start working part-time by giving up that part of the job I found so awful. One coworker, Carl, took it as a personal affront that I had shifted my workload and was upset that I had been granted this arrangement. When my boss was promoted, Carl stepped in as Interim Director and my new supervisor. The first thing he did was tell me that I had to resume the task I disliked so much, and if I didn't, I would be fired.

I had considered entering private practice before, but Carl's directive made it clear to me that now was the time. Yet, at the prospect of leaving my job and the security it offered, I became afraid. What if I failed? What if I couldn't pay my mortgage? How was I going to get clients? When I examined my feelings about starting my own practice, it was clear to me that the idea of staying in my job put me on a downward spiral. My body was telling me I couldn't stay, as I sat, nauseated, at the train station every day after work. My mind was telling me I couldn't stay, as I struggled with anxiety and insomnia every night. Even though I was afraid, the thought of going out on my own filled me with excitement and a sense of adventure at the prospect. I knew it was the right thing to do. Both my fear and my excitement existed at the same time, but it was clear which choice would put me on an upward spiral.

As you learn the fifteen strategies of the POWER Optimism system, you will have the tools you need to make healthy, positive choices for you. Remember, only you can decide what is right for you. The right choice for you is the one that places you on an upward spiral and moves you forward.

> *When you bombard yourself with inward success,*
> *you don't have time to be negative.*
> *—Frank Meyer*

2

Planting Your Power

Chapter Four

Proactive—What Can I Do?

Actively Choosing Responses
Maintaining Personal Accountability
Setting and Achieving Goals

To create success, to promote well-being and to tackle difficulties requires you to take charge. You need to be "response-able" for how you create your life: to be *able to respond* effectively in any given situation. This is the root of being Proactive.

My husband, Jules, began his career as a nurse. He was working in California in 1990 when an earthquake struck. He broke his back in the earthquake and was unable to continue working, especially in the physically demanding field of nursing. As a result, he went on disability benefits for five years. Of course, this was an enormous shock. He became very depressed about what had happened to him both from a physical standpoint and because he had lost his career. When his depression became quite deep, Jules realized that he had to do something to take charge of this situation. He decided to find another type of work. He taught himself computer skills and educated himself on the business (rather than the patient care) side of hospital work. He used these new skills to begin a new career as a health care consultant helping hospitals make their systems run efficiently. His proactive approach didn't end there. Because frequent travel and sitting at a computer makes his back pain worse, he has explored alternative approaches to pain management. He has gotten acupuncture, and he gets a massage every week to help with the discomfort. By being *Proactive*, Jules moved from a downward spiral of depression to an upward spiral of career success and satisfaction.

ACTIVELY CHOOSING RESPONSES

Whenever we are faced with a situation that requires a response, there are three possible arenas in which we can focus our energy and attention: the *No Control Zone*, the *Influence Zone* or the *Control Zone*. If you think about these zones like a target, we want to aim our responses in the Control Zone.

Unfortunately, many of us have a tendency, especially initially, to put all our energy in the No Control Zone. When we are not happy or satisfied with a situation, or when we are feeling frustrated or angry, we go headfirst into the No Control Zone. We can't control things such as the weather or traffic, but we still become stressed when it threatens to snow or there is a traffic jam.

You also can't control what mood your spouse, child, boss or coworkers may be in. Yet how many times do you hear yourself saying, "I want you to," or "Why don't you" or "You should"? These statements tell you you're in the No Control Zone because you want *someone else* to do something, but the reality is you cannot control the thoughts, feelings or actions of another person.

There are two other common No Control Zone responses which you can fall into without even realizing it. When you are obsessed about the past, you are in the No Control Zone. Remember, you can't change the past. When you are worrying about the future, you are also in the No Control Zone, because you cannot predict the future. All of the energy we spend ruminating about the past or fretting about the future is wasted. In fact, you can only take action in the present. Watch for your responses and thoughts that put you in the No Control Zone.

You enter the Influence Zone when you try to affect the outcome of a situation. For example, you can *try* to encourage someone to do something by making a request or presenting your opinion to the other person. Whenever you say, "I would really appreciate if you would do this for me," you are operating in the Influence Zone. Does that mean that the other person *has* to do what you want? No. It doesn't even mean that they *will* do what you want after you've explained it. You can make your needs and wishes known, and the other person can choose to act on that information or not. That's all you can do to let the other person know what's going on with you. Whenever you enter the Influence Zone, it is important not to hold onto expectations about the results. Let your thoughts, feelings and needs be known, and then let go of the results.

The only thing you *always* have control over is your own thoughts, feelings and behaviors. This is the Control Zone. You have control over *your* responses, *your* interpretations and how *you* will handle a situation. You have control over what you will do. To build conditions for success and promote well-being, center your actions on yourself and keep your energy focused in the Control Zone. This is what the *Proactive* Practice is all about: by *actively* choosing your response to a given situation so that you remain in the Control Zone, you can have the most positive impact for yourself. For every specific event, there will be elements that you can control and elements that you cannot. If you're thinking, "This is what I can do," that's good. You're in the Control Zone, and you actually can have an impact and respond in a way that will be successful for you.

> While we may not be able to control all that happens to us,
> we can control what happens inside us.
> —Benjamin Franklin.

When I first went into private practice, I spent a lot of time in the No Control Zone. I worried about what would happen if I didn't get any clients, if no one wanted to hire me as a consultant and if I would make enough money. Lots of terrible images and scenarios played out in my mind: I wouldn't be able to pay the bills; I'd lose my house; I'd be a total failure. Of course, I felt terrible. I then realized that I was completely stuck in the No Control Zone because all I was doing was worrying. My worry was not leading to any productive results, only sleepless nights.

Then I shifted my focus. I thought about what I could influence. In terms of my success with clients, I had responsibility for getting the best training possible and being as good a therapist as possible. I would continue to attend workshops and get supervision. In terms of my success as a businessperson, I could influence building my practice so it would be prosperous. I joined the local Chambers of Commerce and other groups so that I could effectively get the word out about my practice. I taught workshops and classes and advertised my services at those events. I designed and produced materials to help people find me, such as business cards, brochures and posters. None of these things guaranteed that someone would come to me as a client or that a company would hire me as a consultant, even if they saw my materials and heard me speak, but these things helped people learn that I was available and *influenced* their decision to hire me. I saw each of these activities as a positive step towards building a successful practice and as an investment in my future.

By taking charge of my own thoughts, feelings and actions, I moved into the Control Zone. I stopped worrying about the things that were outside of my control, such as the number of clients I had each week. Instead, I began to work on changing my limiting beliefs and schemas that were clouding my vision. I appreciated my efforts to build my business and to invest energy and time in letting people know about what I do. I was grateful that my bills were getting paid, and I truly celebrated every success, no matter how big or small.

Here's another way to show the relationship between your response and your situation:

SITUATION + RESPONSE = OUTCOME

Oftentimes, we must deal with negative situations that are beyond our control to change. In these circumstances, to affect the outcome, you must concentrate on what can be changed *by you*—namely, your response to the situation. It is your response that places you on an upward spiral. Interestingly, we usually think about this in reverse. We assume that the situation itself produces the outcome when in reality it is our responses to that situation that lead to either negative or positive results.

Once I went to conduct a workshop and found that the room wasn't ready and there were twice the number of people I'd been told to expect. That was the situation, and my response was up to me. I was annoyed, of course, but the situation was what it was and I couldn't control it. I knew that if I remained irritated and angry, the workshop would suffer and I wouldn't enjoy the day. Moreover, the people who had come to hear me wouldn't enjoy the day and wouldn't get any benefit from being there for four hours. The outcome was bound to be negative and not helpful for anyone. So, I changed my response from irritation and decided to just let things unfold. I decided my response would be one of spontaneity and that I would enjoy myself no matter what. The workshop was not just successful; it was one of the best I've ever done! By shifting my response, the outcome became positive, and everyone benefited.

Summing Up the Strategy

Actively Choosing Responses involves focusing your attention and awareness on the way you are responding to the people and circumstances in your life. If you find yourself in a situation that cannot be changed, you can choose to *focus on your response* rather than the situation. For example, if you get laid off from your job, you may initially be fearful and angry about the situation, but notice what happens if you shift your focus. You begin to realize that you need a new job and that fear and anger are not the best emotions to motivate a job search. You ask yourself what you can think and do to start networking and generate job leads. In other words, you begin to create actions that can lead to the positive outcome of a new job.

Actively Choosing Responses means *sharing information that will influence the situation and staying detached from the outcome.* You can tell your boss why you deserve a raise, you can share with your mother why her negative attitude bothers you, you can discuss with your teenager why smoking is a health hazard—but you must emotionally and intellectually let go of the outcome. You may not get a raise, your mother may remain negative and your teen may smoke. If you become overly invested in the outcome you desire, your well-being becomes dependent on someone else's behavior, thoughts or feelings. When you stay detached, you recognize that the best you can do is influence the outcome, so you can usually greet any outcome with equanimity and poise.

Finally, *Actively Choosing Responses* requires you to step out of the No Control Zone and to *enter the Control Zone*. When you are in the No Control Zone, you will be wasting your energy and depleting your inner resources. For example, you may be spending time worrying about how much money you'll have for retirement, yet it won't do you any good to worry. When you stop worrying and start taking necessary actions to prepare for the future, such as going to a financial advisor or reading books on investing, you have moved into the Control Zone. If there are no actions to take, you can still choose to stop worrying, recognizing that worrying is fruitless. If you are continuously thinking about the past, you can enter the Control Zone by doing the exercises in Chapter 3 to let go of past events. Remember, you are in the No Control Zone when you look to others to bring you happiness and success. If your spouse is in a bad mood, for example, that doesn't mean you have to take it personally. Your well-being depends not on changing others, but on your own interpretations and reactions to what is happening in the present moment. When you put yourself in the Control Zone, you are creating your own empowerment.

GROWING YOUR PROACTIVE PRACTICE	
Actively Choosing Responses	
GROWTH SLUMP	**GROWTH SURGE**
Focus on the situation.	Focus on your response.
Become overly invested in a certain outcome after sharing information.	Share information to influence situations and stay detached from outcomes.
Enter the No Control Zone • Worry about the future • Obsess about the past • Look to others to change	Enter the Control Zone • Take action in the present • Let go of the past • Look to yourself to choose beneficial reactions

MAINTAINING PERSONAL ACCOUNTABILITY

The way we explain things to ourselves and to others is incredibly important. We can either do so in ways that make us a victim to circumstances, or we can be *Proactive* and recognize our role as active creators of our own lives. This is where *Maintaining Personal Accountability* comes into play. You cannot be empowered if you are unwilling to hold yourself accountable for your own thoughts, feelings and behaviors. The best way to notice if you are giving away your power to other people or not taking charge of your life is by paying attention to your language. The words we choose are a reflection of our thoughts and, in turn, they influence our feelings and behaviors.

Greg came to see me because he was overwhelmed by bitterness about losing his job. He had gone on a long vacation and returned to his office to learn that his boss, who was the firm's development director, had lost a major client and, thus, a large contract. As a result, Greg's position was eliminated, and he was out of a job with almost no warning. He was furious and consumed by anger and self-pity. Greg couldn't understand why this had happened to him and spent enormous amounts of time obsessing about why he had such bad luck, why his boss had been so irresponsible and what a jerk the lost client was.

After working with me, Greg realized that his negative attitude wasn't getting him anywhere. He was giving away all of the responsibility and control over the situation to other people, namely to his boss and the former client. He wasn't taking any responsibility for changing the situation and, therefore, had no power. Greg could continue to blame his boss and keep up his pity party, but the reality was that he needed a new job, and it was unlikely that anyone would want to hire such an angry, bitter and self-righteous person.

With some work, Greg was able to shift his thinking from *"Why is this happening to me?"* to *"What can I do about this situation?"* By accepting personal accountability for his situation and letting go of his anger about it, Greg was able to start moving forward again. He decided to use this opportunity to explore different careers, went on several informational interviews and applied for interesting jobs. Because he was emphasizing his own role in his life (instead of his boss' role), Greg was able to focus on what he wanted out of the situation. He got a new job in a company that is less reliant upon contracts to cover salaries, and he feels more secure about his position.

In Greg's story, it is easy to see the connection between thoughts, feelings and behavior. When Greg was busy blaming his boss, he was generating feelings of anger and hopelessness. His thoughts and feelings acted as a block, preventing him from looking for a new job. As soon as Greg adopted a perspective of personal accountability, he felt energized and became mobilized. He engaged his creative juices to take action and landed a new and even better position.

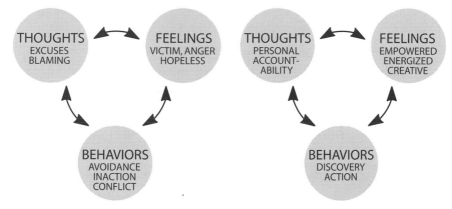

Another client, Larry, had trouble with his financial life. Larry never kept track of his finances, bounced checks all the time and overspent every month. He came to see me because he was feeling overwhelmed by his debt and unable to do anything about it. Larry believed he needed a better-paying job in order to solve his money problems since he didn't think there was any way he could spend less. He explained to me, *"This is how I am. There's nothing I can do about it."* Of course, you already know that Larry was giving away all of his power and taking no responsibility for his own behavior. When he shifted the way he thought to *"I can choose to behave differently,"* Larry got his power back. He was able to examine why he avoided taking charge of financial matters and recognized that he was modeling his behavior after his father. Larry had grown up in a household where his father spent money on whatever he wanted and Larry's mother picked up the pieces. Unconsciously, Larry was duplicating this irresponsible and selfish approach. He also felt deprived because his childhood had been so unstable, and he compensated by rewarding himself whenever he wanted something.

Larry was able to learn another way of behaving and thinking about money. He was able to acknowledge that *he* governed his life and to assume control of his spending. When he decided that he didn't want to repeat his father's problems and that he could live differently, Larry was able to set up a system to balance his checkbook, look at where he was spending his money and start to cut back on his spending. He recognized that he bought a lot of things that weren't very meaningful and he didn't really want anyway. It wasn't as hard as he had expected to curtail his spending and get back on his feet financially. Larry realized that he was his own person with control over his life and stopped ceding responsibility to his father.

In the examples of Greg and Larry, notice the shift in language that each man made. They both moved from interpretations that gave away responsibility for their lives to someone else—Greg's boss and Larry's father. In order to be accountable, you have to take that control back. One way to do this is to stop using statements that push responsibility onto other people or situations. With accountability statements, you operate from an empowered position because you are taking responsibility for your thoughts, feelings and behaviors.

> *Take your life in your own hands, and what happens?*
> *A terrible thing: no one to blame.* —Erica Jong

The list below gives examples of statements that either make *excuses* or promote *accountability*. If your words are operating from the left hand column, you are becoming a victim by giving away your power to take charge of your life. Operating from the accountability side empowers you and allows you to become an active creator of your life.

Excuse	Accountability
I can't do anything about that.	What choices do I have here?
I'm too stupid.	I can learn more.
It's his fault, not mine.	I'm in charge of my life.
You make me mad.	I manage my own feelings.
I've always been this way.	I can create new behaviors.

Language is very influential.[1] Take a moment to just read each sentence in the chart out loud. How does it affect you when you compare an "Excuse" statement with an "Accountability" statement? Most people notice a shift from a downward spiral to an upward spiral when they move into the accountability side.

Summing Up the Strategy

Maintaining Personal Accountability is rooted in taking responsibility for your own role and your own centrality in your life. POWER Optimists are not passive reactors to what happens around them. When you *recognize your active role in creating the outcome you desire*, you take charge of your life. If you aren't prepared to roll up your sleeves and get working on your own life, who will? Pay attention to excuses and rationalizations. If you hear yourself saying, "I can't," change your statement to "I can" and "I will." If you find yourself saying, "Yes, but…" drop the excuse so you can open yourself up to action and options.

When you put the blame on another person, it's easy to lose control of your life. Perhaps your parents failed you in some way or you got passed over for a promotion. It's easy to get caught up in blaming your parents or your supervisor for your unhappiness or lack of success. When you do this, you have diminished your own accountability and reduced your energy. Who wants to be a victim all the time? Instead, concentrate on yourself and your own part in what happens to you. Think about how you are responding to what happens. *Examine your own thoughts, feelings and actions using accountability statements.* You can shift yourself onto an upward spiral by remembering that you are in charge of your adult experience, not your parents. You can learn why you didn't get the promotion and make any necessary changes for the future. When you focus on your accountability, your thoughts, feelings and actions lift you out of victimization towards empowerment.

Maintaining Personal Accountability uses what we know about how the brain works and takes advantage of the fact that thoughts, feelings and actions are all connected. The POWER Optimist *chooses thoughts, feelings and actions that are empowering*, which help to build energy and generate excitement about possibilities that can be made real. The upward spiral this creates will help you change the way your life is going, as Greg did when he used his job crisis as a way to find out what he really wanted to do for a living. Greg stopped feeling like a victim and giving up because he experienced an unexpected setback. Giving up is a surefire way to get on a downward spiral. While you will certainly have disappointments and times when things aren't going your way, you can choose to be empowered by being accountable for your thoughts, feelings and actions.

GROWING YOUR PROACTIVE PRACTICE	
Maintaining Personal Accountability	
GROWTH SLUMP	GROWTH SURGE
Come up with excuses and rationalizations.	Recognize your active role in creating the outcome you desire.
Blame others for your unhappiness or lack of success.	Examine and change your thoughts, feelings and actions using accountability statements.
Feel like a victim and give up.	Choose thoughts, feelings and behaviors that are empowering.

SETTING AND ACHIEVING GOALS

The third strategy for becoming more proactive in your life is setting and achieving goals. By *goals*, I don't mean those items that appear on a "to do" list, such as "return rental videos" or "finish taxes." What I mean by a goal is something that you really *want*, which will bring you joy and move you closer to your dreams. Think big when you're setting your goals, and keep in mind that *goals are not tasks!*

Remember that POWER Optimism is not wishful optimism. POWER Optimists do not focus on unattainable goals. In order to make your goal achievable, distill what you want to its essence. For example, rather than setting the unrealistic goal of "I want to be loved and appreciated by everyone," think about the essence of this statement. The intention of the goal is to experience acceptance and love. Thus, a feasible goal might be to build strong friendships with important people in your life. It is also important to let your goals unfold. Don't become too wedded to a particular concept of image or the goal. Set achievable goals by focusing on what you can accomplish, while at the same time recognizing that life is fluid and new possibilities are always taking shape. The goal of building strong friendships can come about in an infinite number of ways, so hold fast to the intention of your goal, but let go of the form that it might take in reality.

When you're thinking about what your goals might be, ask yourself:

- What do I want to accomplish?
- What do I want to obtain?
- What do I want to contribute?

Once you have determined some goals for yourself, create a plan for getting there. You will need to call upon two strengths: *willpower* and *waypower*.[2] Willpower is the energy and commitment to work towards accomplishing your goals. It is based on thoughts that allow you to initiate and sustain actions, such as "I can," "I'm ready" and "I have what it takes." Willpower helps you sustain momentum over time by giving you positive energy and determination to pursue your goals. Waypower refers to the actual plans you devise to achieve your goals. It is the blue-print or map that guides your actions. You need both of these elements to be successful: waypower is like the car that you're driving to your destination (goal); and willpower is the energy that moves the vehicle.

Take the development of POWER Optimism as an example. I had been designing and leading workshops for employee assistance programs for more than 15 years. I really enjoyed the work I was do-ing, but I always wanted to develop and promote a program of my own that reflected my core beliefs and insights. This was the essence of my goal—to create my own program. I did not yet know what form the program would take, but I was clear about my intention.

I knew that I would have to obtain the credentials and background that would make any program I designed credible, so the first thing I decided was to go back to school and get my Ph.D. This is where will-power came in. In order to go to graduate school, I had to overcome my limiting belief that made me fear I wasn't smart enough to research and write a dissertation. I also had a limiting belief that I was too old to start on such a huge, new undertaking. By this time, luckily, I knew enough that I wasn't going to let these limiting beliefs get in the way. I actively explored the limiting beliefs and reminded myself that I had successful-ly completed two Masters degrees, so there was absolutely no reason I couldn't figure out how to complete a dissertation. I also discovered that there were many older adults in Ph.D. programs, so age was not a rel-evant factor. I engaged my willpower by creating the empowering beliefs of "I can do this" and "This is a new adventure." I kept my willpower active by acting as my own biggest booster and constantly reminded myself that getting a Ph.D. was not only do-able, but would also be fun. This was my willpower, creating the energy to take on the project.

Waypower comes in creating a plan to achieve the goal. My goal had two parts: finishing my dissertation and developing my own pro-gram. When it came time to tackle my dissertation, I began by reading lots of "how to" books. I used the information to build a road map for the project, which was an invaluable guide to accomplishing the many steps involved in the process. It took over two years, but I finally received the title of "Dr. Dana." I then activated my waypower to begin designing my own program. The content of the program developed over time, gradually taking shape as I kept working with various elements. It was an exciting process to see my goal unfold and to watch it take form. After several months, all the elements came together and the concept of POWER Optimism was born. I continued to engage my waypower by first teaching POWER Optimism in an evening school class to test out the materials. I then created a workbook, continuing to refine the materials as I presented workshops and classes. Finally, I expanded the workbook into the book you are now reading.

> *Can't nothin' make your life work if you ain't the architect.*
> —*Terry McMillan*

Each stage of developing and creating POWER Optimism included a million baby steps, each of which moved me closer to success. Both willpower and waypower were essential parts of the process. I engaged my willpower often by using a lot of productive "self-talk" and by continuing to pull the weeds and drop the rocks of my own negative patterns. Waypower was the series of plans and steps which I took in order to accomplish my goal. Both willpower and waypower are like the nutrients in a garden's soil. You can't see them when you're looking at a beautiful, flowering garden, but these nutrients are critical to reaching the goal of having such a flourishing and attractive garden.

It's very important to recognize that while you are moving towards a goal, it is almost inevitable that you will experience setbacks and disappointments. Getting there may well take longer than you expected or hoped. When you experience a setback, remember to keep following the fundamental principle of POWER Optimism—finding an interpretation that will produce an upward spiral. The way you interpret momentary disappointments makes all the difference between following through and trying again or becoming overwhelmed and giving up. Do you think of reaching your goal as an *uphill battle* (a disempowering interpretation) or as a *challenge* (a motivating interpretation)? Do you see setbacks as *failures* (leading to low energy and a strong likelihood of giving up) or *temporary problems* (a high energy interpretation that encourages additional effort)? Choose an interpretation that will keep you on an upward spiral, and use your willpower to create another plan or a new idea that will lead to success if the first plan doesn't work out.

Summing Up the Strategy

Setting and Achieving Goals requires you to first reflect on and crystallize what you want to have happen in your life. Unless you take this first step, you may either fail to set goals or set goals that do not reflect your true wants and desires. When you *set clear goals based on the essence of what you want*, you are able to simultaneously plan and stay open to new possibilities as your goals unfold. Remember, clear goals are achievable goals. If you say your goal is to be "happy" or "successful," it is essential to really visualize what happiness or success looks like to you. Break down your visualization into conceivable outcomes. For example, is happiness having a fulfilling career or owning a new home? Is success graduating from college or learning to play an instrument? If you fail to set a clear goal, you are likely to become overwhelmed or lose your direction, and then wonder what happened.

Setting and Achieving Goals also means *mobilizing your willpower with productive self-talk and interpretation*. Often times, when you set out to accomplish a goal, your limiting beliefs rear up in full force. If you let them take over, they will inhibit your ability to act and achieve what you want. If your goal is to own a new home, for example, listen for any messages in your head that say, "I'll never find what I want," or "What if something goes wrong?" or "I know I'll lose my job as soon as I sign the mortgage papers." This kind of internal self-talk will only get in the way of your achieving success. Once you are mobilized for action, it is also essential that you *utilize your waypower by devising strategies* so you can take action with a clear plan. To own a new home means setting a price range, finding a real estate agent you trust, deciding on a neighborhood and actually looking at houses. Just as a builder needs a blueprint to guide in the construction of a house, you need a strategy to guide your actions in finding a home.

You are not likely to reach your goal the first time you try, so remember that a part of *Setting and Achieving Goals* is to *learn from setbacks and tap into both willpower and waypower to keep motivated*. You can become disheartened when you experience a setback and give up when your progress slows. In my experience of buying a house, I actually started the process three times. The first time I became so overwhelmed by the fear generated by my limiting beliefs, I had to stop looking for a house and simply focus on my willpower—trusting that I was able to be a homeowner. The second time, I didn't have a plan. I didn't know enough about my finances and became discouraged when I didn't see any homes I liked. I took time to learn about mortgages, taxes and hidden expenses, and I focused my search on two neighborhoods. By my third attempt, I was already an experienced house-hunter. I found my home within two weeks, made a bid twenty minutes after seeing the house and have been living there ever since.

GROWING YOUR PROACTIVE PRACTICE	
Setting and Achieving Goals	
GROWTH SLUMP	**GROWTH SURGE**
Fail to set a clear goal.	Set clear goals based on the essence of what you want.
Let your limiting beliefs take over.	Mobilize your willpower with productive self-talk and interpretation.
Take action without a clear plan.	Utilize your waypower by devising strategies.
Give up when progress is slow or setbacks occur.	Learn from setbacks and tap into both willpower and waypower to keep motivated.

Gardening is always more successful when you are proactive. You might not be able to control the weather, but you can take it into account. You may not prevent insect infestation, but you can contain the damage by being prepared. Life is always more successful when you are proactive. You cannot control every event that occurs, but you can choose your reactions wisely. You may not prevent setbacks and losses, but you can limit the consequences by being accountable, and you can certainly ensure that you will thrive by focusing on the needs, wants and desires that you choose to plant in your life's garden.

Chapter Five

Open-minded—What are Innovative Responses?

Searching Out Possibilities
Thinking Expansively
Solving Problems Creatively

Thinking back on the discussion about the way the brain establishes pathways, you'll remember that our brains tend to fall back on patterns that are ingrained and habitual. It's the same in creating conditions for success and well-being: the brain tends to turn to patterns and ways of thinking that are familiar rather than ones that are unusual or innovative. When the brain does this, when it uses well-established pathways, you're likely to get stuck doing the same old thing, which will produce the same old results. To be Open-minded means to bring flexibility to your thinking, expand your vision and act creatively.

Here are three examples from my life in which I practiced being Open-minded. You remember that I enjoy acting and like to take acting classes. Unfortunately, I haven't had a lot of time to take an eight-week course like the ones I had been taking in the past. Still, acting class is an important activity for me, so I decided to be flexible about meeting this need. I searched on the Internet and found an intensive weekend class being offered in my area. This was something I could do, it fit my schedule and it satisfied my "act hunger." In the same manner, when I made the decision to get my Ph.D., I knew I didn't want to attend a traditional program. The thought of going to graduate school full-time, amassing a large debt and sitting in classes with students who had no hands-on experience sent me into a downward spiral. I knew I was looking for an unusual program, but I had confidence I could find one that met my criteria. It took time and a lot of searching, but I found what I wanted. Had I never expanded my vision, I probably would not have discovered such a great Ph.D. program nor had such a terrific experience. Finally, some time ago, I realized I needed to find some kind of satisfying activity that occurred in the middle of the day so that I had a reason to get out of my office before my evening clients. I normally exercised in the morning but decided to shift my routine. As a result of changing my habit, I was able to create a greater sense of well-being by taking time in the middle of the day to do something for me that was not work-related.

As you can see, being *Open-minded* means avoiding habitual ways of addressing problems, working to get out of a rut, and broadening your vision of possibilities. What you're really doing by being Open-minded is waking up your brain, expanding your repertoire of options and increasing your chances of creating success and well-being.

SEARCHING OUT POSSIBILITIES

The most important element in *Searching Out Possibilities* is to believe that possibilities *are* available to you. A person's belief that many possibilities exist is known as having an "abundance attitude" and is one of the major keys to success. An abundance attitude assumes that the world is dynamic and expansive, that there are enough resources and opportunities to go around and that problems can be successfully solved. The opposite view, called a "scarcity mentality," is character-ized by a belief that the world is static and therefore only a limited amount of resources and opportunities exist. The scarcity mentality leads to feelings of fear and anxiety over potential losses and a sense that one person's good fortune is another person's bad luck. Here's a comparison of the two views.

Scarcity Mentality	Abundance Attitude
Limited/fixed resources	Plentiful/available resources
Static worldview	Dynamic worldview
Fear of failure and loss	Trust in success

Research shows that abundance thinking is connected to perseverance.[1] A scientific study looked at the behavior of two groups of rats. One group swam in an opaque pool of water under which a platform was submerged. The second group swam in the same pool, but the hidden platform had been removed. The rats in the first group eventually located the hidden platform and were able to climb up on it to rest. The second group of rats had to swim until they were tired with nowhere to rest. Later, the same rats were put into the pool again, without the hidden platform. The rats from the first group, which had found the hidden platform in the earlier test, swam far longer than the rats that hadn't found a platform in their first test. Why did the first group of rats keep swimming? They *expected* to find a platform, and so they were willing to look for one longer. The second group of rats did not expect to find any platforms, so they didn't persevere as long. The first set of rats had an abundance attitude, and as a result, they persevered and had more stamina.

Of course, we're not rats, but the same kind of attitude works in humans. For people, an abundance framework leads to greater perseverance, better performance and higher expectations for success.[2] One research study found that people who were given candy or praise, or who recalled a happy event (thus creating a good mood and an abundance attitude), set higher goals for themselves, performed better at a given task and persisted longer at the activities at hand. The point is, you have a choice in which viewpoint you want to adopt: an abundance attitude or a scarcity mentality. An abundance attitude helps you operate from the position that there is a solution to your problems and a way of approaching things that will be successful. Unlike a scarcity mentality, an abundance attitude will put you on an upward spiral.

> *If opportunity doesn't knock, build a door.*
> *—Milton Berle*

People who have a scarcity worldview fear that things will never change. Take someone who is looking for a job when the economy is slow. We'll call her Claire. Claire has a static worldview and fears that there aren't as many openings as there would be if the economy were stronger. She is afraid that she'll never get hired and feels dejected about the entire process. When she sees other people getting new jobs, Claire panics, believing that every time someone else gets a job, her own search will be harder since there's one less job opening out there. Other people's success makes her feel even worse, and she believes there is something wrong with her and that she's bound to fail in her attempt to find a new job. When Claire thinks along these lines she gets pulled into a downward spiral, where all her negative thoughts and fears reinforce one another. Her energy level goes down and she feels depressed. The net effect is that it is hard for her to get motivated and keep looking for that next job. Her fears, in essence, become her reality.

A POWER Optimist who is looking for a job, on the other hand, has a dynamic worldview. She is *Open-minded* and chooses a different interpretation of the job search process. We'll call this POWER

Optimist Barbara. Barbara uses the strategy of *Searching Out Possibilities*. She knows that she only needs *one* job. Barbara believes that, regardless of the state of the economy, one job is out there. Her task is to find the most appropriate employer to hire her. She's not looking to turn the economic forecasts for the whole country around; she just needs one little job. Barbara can think of lots of things she'd be good at and is interested in exploring them. When she sees other people getting new jobs, Barbara recognizes this fact as a sign that people get hired every day, which means that jobs are being filled. She could be next. Being *Open-minded* moves Barbara along an upward spiral; she is energized and engaged by her job hunt. Because the process takes her on an upward spiral, the good feelings reinforce her behavior, and it is easier for Barbara to keep looking for a new job than it is for Claire.

Summing Up the Strategy

Searching Out Possibilities asks you to *focus on what you want or desire*. This is an inherently optimistic frame of mind that takes you on an upward spiral. *Searching Out Possibilities* avoids focusing on lacks or deficits, which can cause you to cycle downward and lead to inertia and depression. In the example above, Barbara focuses on what she wants to have happen (getting a new job) and is energized to pursue that goal. Claire, on the other hand, focuses on the fact that she lacks a job and the economy isn't great. Her mindset interferes with the energy she needs to pursue her goal of getting a new job. Remember, you always have a choice in how you focus your attention. If you notice yourself thinking or talking about what you lack, shift your focus.

Searching Out Possibilities involves *operating from an abundance attitude*. This viewpoint is more likely to take you on an upward spiral as compared to a scarcity mentality. For example, suppose you need more money but your company isn't giving out raises this year. You say to yourself, "The problem is my company didn't make enough profit to give me a pay increase." Now, this statement is making the assumption that there is a limited supply of money, so you can't get any extra. This perspective can easily stop your brain from firing up and thinking creatively and may even send you into a downward spiral. Instead, you might say to yourself, "My company isn't giving out raises this year, so in what ways can I get more money?" This shift in perspective assumes that more money is available and you simply need to find a way to tap into the money stream. Neither perspective can guarantee you'll get more money, but an abundance attitude will fire up your creative juices and open the doors of possibility.

Searching Out Possibilities also entails *keeping yourself open to favorable outcomes.* Rather than letting fears and anxieties dictate your choices and limit your horizons, be open to possibilities that arise. My friend Jesse's mother is a great example of a person who moved from fear to openness. Jesse's father died, and after his mother had mourned for what was—for her—an appropriate amount of time, she started looking for ways to spend her energy and re-create her life. She joined a number of clubs so that she could explore her hobbies and became an active member of her community. She missed her husband, but she knew that it was possible for her to find ways to enjoy herself and be connected to other people around her. At the age of 79, she fell in love with a man she met at church, and remarried. She told Jesse, "I'm so happy that I overcame my fears and decided to go on with my life. It was hard at first to meet new people and do different things, but it's never too late for a new beginning. It's never too late for new things to happen to you!"

GROWING YOUR OPEN-MINDED PRACTICE	
Searching Out Possibilities	
GROWTH SLUMP	**GROWTH SURGE**
Focus on a perceived lack.	Focus on what you want or desire.
Interpret situations from a scarcity mentality.	Operate from an abundance attitude.
Let fear of loss or failure cloud your perception.	Keep yourself open to favorable outcomes.

THINKING EXPANSIVELY

Wake up your brain! *Thinking Expansively* is the second strategy in the *Open-minded* Practice. It means thinking outside the box, thinking creatively, using your imagination. How often do you notice that you are doing something on auto-pilot, not really paying attention? How often do you do things in the same routine, such as driving to work, doing the dishes or making meals? When our brains are so sure of the routine, they become glazed over. The fact is, we go through life with our brains half asleep.

Thinking Expansively is the process of waking up your brain so you can create more interesting and imaginative options in your life. You can start waking up your brain in very simple ways. Change your route to work or the way you go through your grocery store. These simple changes shake up your routine and make your brain more attentive. Brush your teeth with your non-dominant hand. Walk down a street and find three things you've never noticed before. For example, a while ago, after I'd lived in the same house for 10 years, I decided to look for three new things on my block. Right away, I noticed that my neighbor, Joe, had a beautiful stained glass window in the front of his house. The next time I saw Joe I asked when he'd put it in. "What are you talking about?" Joe said, looking at me like I was crazy. It turned out that the window had been there for 30 years, but I had never noticed it. By going out looking for new things, I had "seen" something that had been there all along!

Thinking Expansively acknowledges that there are many options available to us, although we often mistakenly believe that there are only a limited number of possibilities. *Thinking Expansively* allows us to generate new ways of perceiving a problem or situation by looking at more aspects of it and by bringing our mental creativity into play. Mental creativity has three components: originality, fluency and flexibility.[3]

- **Originality**: *Generating ideas without censoring them.* Writing your ideas down and considering them, no matter how strange, implausible or wacky they may seem, is worthwhile. This is because at the margins of ideas that are unworkable or impractical, you may identify something really worth pursuing.

- *Fluency*: *Producing numerous ideas in a set amount of time.* Coming up with ideas at a rapid pace, for a certain period of time, can help spark new ideas. When your brain is working quickly and consistently, it gets fired up and the creative energy starts to flow.

- *Flexibility*: *Being willing to not only think outside the box, but to live outside the box as well.* When you are willing to try something new, you will experience zestfulness accompanied by feelings of excitement, purpose and passion. These emotions combine to take you on an upward spiral and generate even more new thoughts and attitudes.

By working to strengthen these three components, you can increase your mental creativity.

All of these characteristics are tapped when one engages in "brainstorming." Brainstorming is the term that describes the process of generating any and all ideas about a subject or situation. It means getting all of your ideas about a particular problem or issue out on the table, without censorship, and only considering them later on. In brainstorming, the goal is to let your ideas flow without stopping to judge their merits or practicality. Brainstorming taps into all three factors of mental creativity, and helps address underlying issues as well as surface problems.

When brainstorming, it's critical to approach any situation as if you had unlimited resources. In other words, it is important to adopt an abundance attitude. By accepting this perspective, you are free to generate *all* the available possibilities and move beyond your habitual belief systems. Accepting limitations, making judgments and censoring ideas in a brainstorming exercise are really just examples of thinking inside the box and will keep you from coming up with new ideas. When you hear yourself say "but…" stop right there. Ignore the objection you were about to make, whether it was about time, money, skills or some other perceived lack, and move back to thinking of ideas, however implausible, expensive or time-consuming. In brain-storming, all options are possible and must be listed.

> *Look for opportunity. You can't wait for it to knock on the door…*
> *you might not be at home.*
> *—Jinger Heath*

Here's a brainstorming exercise I use in my workshops. Suppose Tony, a 67-year-old man, goes for his annual checkup. His doctor tells Tony that he has a heart condition and must take it easy. It's summer-time and Tony has a large lawn which he is very proud of. He knows that following his doctor's orders means he can't mow the lawn over the summer, but he doesn't think he can afford to pay a service to mow it for him. What should he do? Take a couple of minutes to think about Tony's dilemma. What usually happens when I give this story at a workshop, is that people come up with a lot of really creative ways that Tony can solve his problem. Here are just a few of them:

- Borrow a sheep from a local farmer to eat the grass.
- Trade homebaked bread or cakes for lawn-mowing services.
- Let the yard go wild for the summer.
- Ask his children to help him mow the lawn.
- Check civic organizations and see if they can do it.
- Get a second medical opinion.
- Borrow or buy a riding mower.
- Cover the lawn with plastic sheeting.
- Live somewhere else that summer.

Some of the ideas that are generated might actually work for Tony. Some of them wouldn't. The point is to let the ideas flow and accumulate without processing them. You can go back and assess them later.

One of my clients, Francine, was tired of her teaching job and trying to find a new position. She started feeling really hopeless and depressed about it, though, when she realized she typically circled other teaching and educational job listings in the newspaper. These all seemed very similar to the job she already had. Francine wasn't really interested in another teaching job, but she didn't know what else she wanted to do for a living. She kept falling back on using the skills she knew she had, her teaching skills, rather than thinking bigger about the skills she was interested in gaining. We decided to *Think Expansively* about her job search and brainstorm about her situation.

Practicing mental creativity, Francine harnessed her originality, fluency and flexibility. Using *originality*, she worked to come up with as many ideas as she could, without censoring any of them. Some of her ideas seemed wacky to her (like trapeze artist, writer, massage therapist), but she let them flow. At first, Francine was reluctant to really put down her most far-fetched ideas; she tried to censor herself so she wouldn't feel foolish about some of her thoughts. She worked against this fear and began being more *fluent*, working consistently for 20 minutes, steadily generating possibilities. When her ideas began to flag, Francine kept thinking, and her brain revved up again. Over the next few minutes, her list grew rapidly. Because she was thinking expansively, Francine was able to think outside the box and her list included many different kinds of ideas and occupations.

Next, she and I picked three professions from the list. These were areas Francine thought she might like to learn more about. Notice that she didn't commit right then and there to taking a job in one of these three areas; she was just exploring at this point. This is an important facet of *flexibility*—the willingness to explore new things. Francine's top three alternate careers were: professional organizer (someone who helps people create more appealing and less cluttered living spaces), social worker and acupuncturist. Over the next several months, Francine arranged informational interviews with people from each of these fields. She reworked her resume and created different versions that were appropriate for these careers and read a lot about these kinds of work. She took classes and visited people's offices to see what their working environments were like.

Francine didn't quit her teaching job immediately, but she's no longer anxious about it. This has been a time of reflection and exploration for her, and she wants to take her time and make a good decision. She knows that the best outcomes are often the ones that take the most work. Because she has been thinking flexibly about the career shift, she's been energized by the process rather than demoralized and depressed. She enjoys teaching more, also, because she doesn't feel trapped. While Francine hasn't achieved her goal yet, she is working to get there and feeling good about the process.

Summing Up the Strategy

If you want to practice *Thinking Expansively, shake up your routines regularly*. The opposite approach is to go through life on auto-pilot, never altering your routines nor exploring new behaviors. Following the same old ways of doing things can keep you stuck in a rut, which leads to a lack of energy and a downward spiral. Experimenting with new behaviors helps shift you to an upward spiral, where you can become energized by your experiences. You may be so busy and over-scheduled in your life that it can be hard to think about changing your routine, but the change may be just the lift your spirits need. It doesn't matter what you do, just do something different! Eat your next meal with your non-dominant hand. Change the order of your morning and evening grooming. Go to a movie at an unusual time. Any of these behaviors will shake up your routine and wake up your brain.

Thinking Expansively also means that you *commit to developing your mental creativity*. Watch children at play. It is evident that their ability to be resourceful and creative comes naturally. You have that same innate inventiveness, but it may have become dampened over time. Rev up your mental creativity by solving puzzles, playing charades or Pictionary, creating "life stories" for strangers you see, playing games with children, or writing a story or play. By nurturing your imagination, it will be ready to serve you when you need to tap into your originality.

Finally, make sure you *approach new possibilities with a sense of curiosity*. Francine didn't look at the career ideas she brainstormed with a closed mind. Instead, she stayed open to exploring possibilities outside her box of teaching by being curious about what these other jobs were like. Curiosity is your ally in *Thinking Expansively* because it helps you remain open and flexible. Ask questions. Be inquisitive. Talk to people. By engaging your inner explorer, you're ensuring you will move beyond your routine thoughts into uncharted territory.

GROWING YOUR OPEN-MINDED PRACTICE	
Thinking Expansively	
GROWTH SLUMP	**GROWTH SURGE**
Conduct your life on auto-pilot.	Shake up your routines regularly.
Stick to the same ideas you've always had.	Commit to developing your mental creativity.
Look at new ideas with a closed mind.	Approach new possibilities with a sense of curiosity.

SOLVING PROBLEMS CREATIVELY

Imagine Maureen, a mother of two small daughters, finding her children fighting over an orange. She grabs the orange, slices it in half, and gives each girl the same-sized piece. "There," she thinks, "problem solved!" Far from being satisfied, both girls are unhappy! It turns out that one had wanted to eat the fruit, and the other wanted to make boats out of the peel to play with in her bath. While Maureen was dealing with a relatively minor problem in the large scheme of things, her failure to actually solve the problem illustrates what happens when we respond to problems in ordinary and habitual ways. Success and well-being are more likely to result when you employ the third strategy of being Open-minded: *Solving Problems Creatively*.

Creative problem solving is a cycle, one that continuously feeds back on itself. Here's a model that shows how this works:

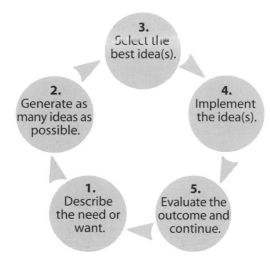

Circle 1: Describe the need or want. It's important to dig down and identify the *underlying* need or want represented by the problem at hand. Remember, the problem that appears to you may not be the real issue, as with Maureen and her daughters. To start identifying the needs, issues and wants that are the root of the problem, ask yourself these basic questions:

- What need do I have here?
- What do I want to have happen?
- What issues are underneath the problem?

Let's look at how this works in real life. Carla was depressed about how much weight she'd put on since moving to a new city, and she was thinking about getting liposuction. She defined her problem as, "I'm fat and unattractive, which is making me depressed." She identified the solution to her problem as liposuction. "Liposuction will fix my weight problem, and then I won't be so depressed." But when Carla asked herself the three questions above, she made a startling discovery. She realized that she wasn't depressed because she was overweight; she was overweight because she was depressed, and she was depressed because she was lonely. Since Carla had moved to a new city where she didn't know anyone, she was spending her evenings watching TV and eating junk food. She didn't get any exercise, and she didn't go out because she was unfamiliar with, and intimidated by, her new home. Carla was heavier than she'd like to be, that was true, but the underlying problem in her life was not her weight, but her loneliness and lack of connectedness in her new city.

Circle 2: Generate as many ideas about the solution as you can. Brainstorming as many ideas as possible helps you tap into unusual, innovative, fun and feasible ways to address problems. Remember that true brainstorming means generating as many ideas as you can, regardless of how crazy or inappropriate they seem. It is important to write down your ideas as you're brainstorming so you can refer to the list in creating a solution.

Carla sat down with a pad of paper and the weekly newspaper. She set herself a half hour in which to come up with as many ideas as she could about ways to cure her loneliness and get more engaged in her new home town. When she got blocked or ran out of ideas, Carla took a moment to leaf through the paper and see if anything jumped out at her. Her ideas for solutions to her problem included activities such as taking cooking classes, hiking with a nature-walking club, joining a gym, moving back to her hometown, volunteering for Habitat for Humanity, taking a tour of the city, ushering at a theater, joining a book club, socializing with her co-workers, visiting museums, going to a book discussion at a local book store and placing a personal ad for friends.

Circle 3: Select the best idea(s). The next step is to go through the large list of ideas that you generated and think about the ones that are most appealing. Pick a couple of things that seem interesting to you and give them a try. It may seem scary to start on one of them, but remember that trying something is just that—trying it. You are not required to commit to something forever because you started it. In fact, as you'll see, part of creative problem-solving is knowing you can always go back and revisit an idea or an action if the current one doesn't work out.

Carla looked at her list and chose three things to do. She decided to join a gym near her house to help lift her mood and get some exercise, to become a member of a local hiking club so she could meet new people and discover the area's natural resources and to start socializing with people at her office by inviting them to lunch with her. By selecting the best ideas on the list, Carla felt excited and eager to try out her solutions.

Circle 4: Implement the idea(s). The next step is to actually try out the ideas that are on the "short list" and see how they work out. It may take time to really implement them, but that's OK. The process of starting something and working on it can be rewarding in itself.

Carla called a gym right away and joined that week. She took a couple of classes, decided that she liked spinning the best and settled into a routine of taking a couple of spinning classes every week. She started to get to know other regulars in the class and was pleased when she ran into them around her neighborhood. Carla also decided to have lunch with everyone in her department, and she set herself a schedule of one lunch every week. She approached a co-worker who seemed really friendly and set up lunch with her later in the month. Finally, Carla looked up hiking clubs in the paper and contacted one for more information on membership and activities.

Circle 5: Evaluate the outcome and continue. The final step in the chain is to assess how well the ideas worked out and decide if you want to stick with the original ideas you tried, add other possibilities or switch tactics. As I said, trying something is not a permanent commitment; it's just exploration. You might want to go back to the list of brainstormed activities and pick another idea to implement, or you might decide that things are going well with the steps you've taken. Every situation is different, and by approaching each one with flexibility, you'll gain the most benefits.

After several months, Carla evaluated her plan. She realized she was feeling a lot better about herself, her weight and her new city. Her weight hadn't changed much yet, but that was no longer her focus. Because she was going to the gym regularly, she wasn't spending as much time at home alone in front of the TV, and she had started making friends at the gym. She had gone to lunch with several people from work and started to get to know them on a more personal level. This also helped her feel more connected. As she got to know her co-workers, they started inviting her to community events outside of work. She accepted their invitations as often as she could and was starting to learn more about goings-on in the town. Finally, Carla had joined the hiking club and gone on several day hikes with the group. As a result of these activities, Carla was feeling less depressed.

In looking at the activities she'd explored over the several months, Carla realized that there were other things from her brainstorming list that she'd like to try. She enjoyed the gym and her co-workers lunches, so she decided to keep up with those activities, but she hadn't really liked hiking as much as she had expected, so she decided to drop out of the club and take a photography class instead. The newspaper had an advertisement for a community art school that offered both classes and lectures, so Carla thought she'd give them a call. When Carla shifted the way she thought about the problems in her life, she was able to address the true issues and to generate and implement creative solutions. Carla's creative problem-solving gave her hope and energy, and took her on an upward spiral.

Summing Up the Strategy

Solving Problems Creatively involves focusing on the underlying issue or need, rather than the problem as it might first appear to be. By searching for the issue underlying your problem, you will be better able to address it and find a solution that will create conditions for success and well-being. Suppose you want to go back to school but decide you don't have enough time. To address the underlying issue, you might ask yourself, "What do I want to have happen?" Your need might be to get a degree, or it might be to be with people or find a source of personal enrichment. Or suppose you describe a problem as not having enough money for a vacation. Ask yourself, "What need do I have here?" Is your need for more money, rest and relaxation, time off from work, travel or to get away from the kids? The need you identify will determine how you go about brainstorming a solution.

Solving Problems Creatively works best when you recognize that there are many possible solutions to a problem. Avoid the trap of believing there is only one right solution. This belief shuts down creativity, limits options and produces undue stress to find the perfect answer. If you find yourself unable to generate options, it is helpful to let go of expectations, explore the problem from a new perspective and draw on your sense of humor. Sometimes, you just have to put the search for a solution aside for a time and give your mind a rest. It's amazing the number of times that an idea or solution will present itself when you're not actively searching for it!

Finally, *Solving Problems Creatively* means keeping the process going. By *evaluating the outcome in order to implement new solutions as needed*, you will be able to make adjustments to your course of action. If you choose a course of action and then stick with it regardless of how it goes, you are practicing dogmatic optimism—not accepting or acknowledging negative information. Even if a solution works well at first, the creative problem solver knows that things can change. People's lives and their situations vary with time, and what works at one point may not work forever. Carla thought that she would enjoy all of the ideas that she tried, but she didn't. Rather than forcing herself to keep up with the hiking club, dogmatically sticking with her original plan, Carla reassessed and changed what she was doing. She stopped doing the things that threatened to put her on a downward spiral and invested her time and energy instead on ideas and actions that placed her on an upward spiral.

GROWING YOUR OPEN-MINDED PRACTICE Solving Problems Creatively	
GROWTH SLUMP	**GROWTH SURGE**
Focus on the problem.	Focus on the need or issue.
Believe that there is only one right solution.	Recognize that there are many possible solutions.
Stop the problem-solving process after a solution has been decided upon.	Evaluate the outcome in order to implement new solutions as needed.

The creative use of trees, flowers, shrubs and grasses in the garden is limitless. Similarly, life offers us options which we can combine in unending possibilities to create our lives. It is only our own limited vision that prevents us from imagining and using the opportunities that exist. If we keep our blinders on, we will only see to the edges of our own self-imposed boundaries. When we expand our vision, we are open to endless innovation.

Chapter Six

Well-informed—What Do I Need to Know?

Appraising Information Objectively
Using Both Reason and Intuition
Taking Intentional Risks

At the heart of *Well-informed* is the practice of gathering and utilizing information. Information is only useful if it can help you reach productive conclusions. Information that is biased, misrepresented, limited or irrelevant will hamper your growth and your ability to create positive outcomes. To be *Well-informed* means becoming self-aware and neutrally observing both the situations around you and your reactions to them. Gathering and objectively assessing all of the information you need helps you not only to eliminate negative filters that can affect your judgment but also to avoid tunnel vision that can limit your outlook. Being *Well-informed* involves using both intuition and reason so you can tap into your full wisdom. When you are *Well-informed*, you can take appropriate risks and make effective decisions that will lead to success and well-being.

In the 1950s, my father started a company that sold television vacuum tubes. In those days, television sets relied on a variety of vacuum tubes to work, and these tubes frequently needed to be replaced. My father's company installed machines in drugstores, where people could test the tubes to see if they needed to be replaced and, if so, buy the new tube from the same machine. How did my father start and grow this business? He took a risk based on his business wisdom. TV tube testers were a new concept, but my father was able to test his ideas before investing significant amounts of money. Once he knew the business was viable, he went all out to make it a success. Then, TV technology changed. Tubes were replaced with transistors. Fortunately, my father looked at the big picture, and he could see this shift occurring. Because he was well-informed, he was able to adapt to keep his business afloat. He changed his business to one that provided battery sales instead of TV tube sales. He already had the infrastructure and the relationships with the drugstores, so he was able to pull out of the tube business and move into providing Eveready and Duracell sales racks. In the end, he was very successful in both the tube and battery business because he practiced the *Well-informed* strategies.

APPRAISING INFORMATION OBJECTIVELY

In some circumstances, limited information is worse than no information at all. Focusing on a single aspect, characteristic or idea will prevent you from understanding the whole situation. *Appraising Information Objectively* involves looking at the big picture and drawing conclusions based on its entirety. This poem is one of my favorite stories because it so clearly illustrates how you can get into trouble by drawing conclusions from only a single feature rather than the entire picture.

The Parable of the Blind Men and the Elephant

John Godfrey Saxe (1816-1887)

It was six men of Indostan
To learning much inclined,
Who went to see the Elephant
Though all were blind,
That each by observation
Might satisfy his mind.

The First approached the Elephant
And, happening to fall
Against his broad and sturdy side,
At once began to bawl;
"God bless me but the Elephant
Is very like a wall!"

The Second, feeling the tusk,
Cried, "Ho! What have we here,
So very round and smooth and sharp?
To me, 'tis very clear
This wonder of an Elephant
Is very like a spear!"

The Third approached the animal
And, happening to take
The squirming trunk within his hands,
Thus boldly up he spake:
"I see," quoth he, "The Elephant
Is very like a snake!"

The Fourth reached out an eager hand,
And felt about the knee:
"What most the wondrous beast is like
Is very plain," quoth he;

"Tis clear enough the Elephant
Is very like a tree!"

The Fifth, who chanced to touch the ear,
Said, "Even the blindest man
Can tell what this resembles most;
Deny the fact who can:
The marvel of the Elephant
Is very like a fan!"

The Sixth no sooner had begun
About the beast to grope
Than, seizing on the swinging tail
That fell within his scope,
"I see," quoth he, "the Elephant
Is very like a rope!"

And so these men of Indostan
Disputed loud and long,
Each in his own opinion
Exceeding stiff and strong.
Though each was partly in the right,
They all were in the wrong!

Looking at only one aspect of something limits your direct experience to a small part of the whole. You are likely to misjudge the situation because you don't understand it objectively. If you appraise information using "tunnel vision," the tendency to examine only a small part of a picture and ignore the larger view, you may be partially right, but chances are you will also be drawing an incorrect conclusion, diminishing the possibility that you will experience success or well-being.

For example, when I first began in private practice, I would use money as a marker of success. That's a prime example of using tunnel vision rather than looking at the big picture. I was not making as much money as I had when I worked for a big company, and according to my financial assessment, I felt like a failure. When I looked at the *whole* picture, though, I got a very different sense of my worth. I could appreciate the value that comes from doing work I love that is incredibly fulfilling. I could see the value that comes from having my own business and being really engaged in what I do. Today, when I fall into the same money trap and feel like a failure because my income isn't in the top bracket, I step back even further to see an even bigger picture. I see the personal wealth that comes from my friendships and marriage, my hobbies and my community. There is so much more going on in my life than just my income. When I look at more than the small picture, I can see how very blessed and successful I am.

> When a pickpocket meets a saint,
> all he sees are the pockets.
> —Indian saying

To *Appraise Information Objectively*, it is important to be a neutral observer—to watch what is happening without bringing judgment or bias to the scene. A neutral observer notes his or her reactions to what is happening without getting pulled into an emotional response to the situation. This is known as *detachment*, avoiding becoming enmeshed in a situation or attached to a particular outcome. Being detached doesn't mean that you don't *care* about what's happening. Rather, being a neutral observer involves paying attention to the facts as they are presented through your senses and just accepting these facts in a nonjudgmental manner. Think about the way teachers or therapists observe and assess without emotional involvement. Because they stay above the fray and maintain objectivity, these professionals can see the big picture and make valid recommendations for improvement to their students and clients.[1]

You can acquire this same kind of objectivity by being aware of what is called your *perceptual position*.[2] When you are in the *Self* position, you see other people and the world through your own eyes. In the *Other* position, you experience the world from some other person's viewpoint, taking into account the values, beliefs and emotions of that person. From the *Observer* position, you experience the world from the outside, as if you were viewing characters and events in a film. By deciding to step outside yourself and adopt the observer position, you are promoting detachment, objectivity and neutrality.

Being a neutral observer helps you choose your reactions and intentionally process information to draw productive conclusions based on what is going on around you.

A neutral observer is:

- free from judgment and bias
- emotionally disengaged
- unattached to any particular outcome

One year, my husband Jules and I agreed not to buy each other any Valentine's Day presents. Later, I realized that although a present wasn't important to me, I still wanted a card. I talked about this with Jules, but at the time, he had been really busy at work and somewhat overwhelmed. I don't think he was really paying that much attention when I brought this up. Anyway, I went off and got a really great card for him and was feeling very pleased with myself. On Valentine's Day, we spent the evening in and made a nice dinner together. At one point while we were cooking, I said, "OK, let's exchange cards now." He looked at me like I was crazy and said, "What card? Didn't we agree we weren't going to get each other anything this year?" Of course, what happened was that he hadn't remembered our conversation about the cards. But I did.

While Jules was feeling really guilty about not buying me a card, I was starting to get emotionally hijacked. Fortunately, I was able to pull back and engage my neutral observer. When I looked at the situation as if from outside, I was able to recognize that the feelings I was having were old feelings about abandonment and rejection. These emotions were connected to other men who hadn't given me cards or presents for Valentine's Day. My neutral observer remembered that those men were not Jules and that Jules was different and really loved me. The neutral observer noted that Jules may not have bought me a card, but he was cooking dinner for me and does many wonderful things with and for me. My neutral observer was able to stop the emotional hijack by looking at the bigger picture beyond the issue of the card itself. I suggested to Jules that an even better gift than a card would be for him to tell me what a Valentine's Day card from him might say, and he was wonderful. He said all kinds of great things that were really meaningful to me, and the sentiment was just as real as if it had come in a card. He felt better, I felt better and we had a great night. (I did clarify, however, that the *next* Valentine's Day, I wanted us both to exchange cards!)

In order to *Appraise Information Objectively*, it's important not to let your past experiences or fears about the future create your interpretation of an event or situation. You can't be objective and detached if filters influence your perceptions and interfere with your neutrality. Preconceived ideas, concepts and assumptions get in the way of your ability to understand and use new information effectively, and block you from being a neutral observer. If you find that you are unable to be your own neutral observer—free from bias, emotionally detached and unattached to an outcome—find someone who is impartial and can act as a neutral observer for you. Ask for a reality check.

For example, many of my clients come to me with body image issues, thinking that they are too fat, too skinny or just not perfect enough to meet the demands of our youth- and weight-obsessed culture. How many times have you heard a woman complain about her weight or some other part of her body that's not quite right? For men, the corollary feeling is often one of insecurity about their muscularity, strength or baldness. As a therapist and neutral observer, I provide these clients with a reality check. I encourage them to recognize that magazine and movie images of models and stars are often digitally altered for greater effect. No one can expect to look like an image that's been enhanced, cropped, stretched and otherwise manipulated. I invite them to observe real bodies of real people in the real world for comparison, instead of looking at manipulated images for their sense of what's normal. I remind them that having a "perfect" body is no guarantee of happiness. I provide a reality check that allows them to experience and appreciate their full selves and lives.

Summing Up the Strategy

Maintaining a detached and objective view of the big picture is a primary characteristic of *Appraising Information Objectively*. Rather than focusing on a single feature, aspect or characteristic of a situation, *use a wide-angle lens to see all aspects of the situation*. For example, suppose you are looking for a job, have sent out resumes weekly, had several interviews but still have not landed a new position. What's the problem? The information you need to know to answer this question comes from considering all aspects of the situation. Perhaps your resume needs to be rewritten, or maybe there is a problem with your cover letter. It could be you need coaching to improve your interview skills. Perhaps you need to network rather than solely send out resumes. Taking an even longer-range view, you might consider whether you qualify for the kind of position you are seeking. By assessing all these possibilities, the conclusions you reach and the decisions you make are more likely to be productive and lead to your getting a new job.

Part of *Appraising Information Objectively* is remaining detached. When you *operate as a neutral observer*, you are able to make much more informed and thoughtful decisions. Looking at information through the lens of your negative patterns, on the other hand, creates distractions and assumptions that can get in the way of seeing things clearly. As you continue to work on releasing your negative patterns, it is less likely you will become distracted by fears and anxieties that may come from limiting beliefs, past experiences, schemas or emotional hijacks. If I had assessed information from the perspective of my amygdala when Jules didn't get me a Valentine's Day card, the entire evening would have been ruined. Instead, by maintaining neutrality, I was able to appraise the situation objectively and keep his forgetfulness in perspective. The end result was a great evening that put us both on an upward spiral.

Finally, when *Appraising Information Objectively*, it may be necessary to *get an impartial reality check to encourage an unbiased perspective*. With an impartial reality check, you are more able to make decisions from an objective point of view rather than assessing information based on your preconceptions, assumptions and judgments. Depending on the circumstances, it may be difficult to become your own neutral observer and move beyond assumptions, emotional reactions or past experiences to truly gauge information on its own merits. When this is the case, find someone who is not personally involved in the situation or invested in the outcome. You might ask a trusted friend, spouse or significant other, family member, clergy or co-worker, or you can turn to a psychotherapist, counselor or coach. Getting a reality check can provide just the information you need to move in a forward direction.

GROWING YOUR WELL-INFORMED PRACTICE	
Appraising Information Objectively	
GROWTH SLUMP	**GROWTH SURGE**
Focus on a single feature, aspect or characteristic of a situation.	Use a wide-angle lens to see all aspects of the situation.
Become caught up in negative patterns.	Operate as a neutral observer.
Use preconceptions, assumptions and judgments when assessing information.	Get an impartial reality check to encourage an unbiased perspective.

USING REASON AND INTUITION

POWER Optimists are *whole-brained*. This means they use both the left hemisphere of the brain—which is in charge of reason and logic, and the right hemisphere—which governs creativity and intuition. Using *both* reason and intuition to gather information and make decisions gives you the benefit of the maximum amount of information.

Reason is concerned with accuracy and facts. We use reason to gather logical evidence about the specific details of a situation. Reason is less concerned with the big picture. Reason helps us to compare and contrast data and to analyze details that may affect a situation. Students writing research papers use reason. They look up facts in reference books, gather expert opinions on the topic and organize their thoughts logically so as to be easily understood. Objective facts and statistics are all about reason—where is the tallest building, who is the mayor, are the plates in the dishwasher clean? Reason answers these types of questions. It's pretty easy to tell if a decision based on reason is correct or not because the answer is factual and concrete.

Intuition, on the other hand, is concerned with your own internal and unconscious sense of what's right for you. We use our intuition in relatively minor ways all the time. When you know it's the right time to make that important phone call or you have the urge to check a particular time or date, that's your intuition at work. Intuition is used to gather information about the big picture—intuition is subjective and less concerned with details. When you have a "gut feeling," that's your intuition providing feedback. Intuition synthesizes the body, mind and spirit to bring insight, imagination, feeling and emotion to a decision. It's harder to tell if an intuitive decision is correct because the answers are not factual. You can assess it pretty clearly, though, by checking to see if your decision placed you on an upward or downward spiral. A decision that's correct for your intuition leads to feelings of engagement and excitement. Your decision will feel "right" internally, and you will be on an upward spiral. When you ignore your intuition, you feel as if you are not doing something right, that you are making a mistake. You will feel yourself going along the downward spiral.

Reason	Intuition
Logical	Random
Sequential	Holistic
Rational	Subjective
Analyzes	Synthesizes
Parts	Wholes
Accuracy	Feeling

Here's an example. When I was first out of graduate school, I had a job at a company that provided social services and psychotherapy to patients at local hospitals. The head of the company, Winston, relied on one hospital for our biggest contract and didn't worry about client development. Things seemed to be going along fine until the hospital didn't renew our contract. They went with another company, and we no longer had them as a client. Since the hospital had provided most of our income, the company failed, and we all lost our jobs. It was a real blow, but I found another job. Some time later, I was thinking about leaving that position and looking for something new. Out of the blue, Winston approached me and asked if I'd like to be his partner in a new business venture he was starting. In my gut, I knew that working with him again was a bad idea, but I talked myself into it. I was so determined to leave my current position for something new that I didn't really listen to my inner voice, which was telling me to hold off and make a more considered decision. Instead, I acted impulsively and renewed my relationship with Winston. In the end, this was not a positive decision. Although I was supposed to be his partner, I never was Winston's equal. Our business relationship gradually deteriorated until we parted company. I had ignored my intuition and acted impulsively to satisfy my desire for a new job, even though I could *feel* that the decision was not a good one, and I was heading along a downward spiral.

Scientific research shows that intuition is a real form of knowledge and an essential part of effective decision-making. OK, you're wondering; if I have an internal feeling about wanting to do something like yell at my boss, have that piece of cheesecake or not attend my friend's birthday party, I should go ahead and do it because it is a decision based on my intuition? Not exactly. Those feelings are probably impulses, and there's a big difference between intuition and impulse.[3] When an *impulse* is present, the feeling that you have to act is very strong and pressing. An impulse creates a feeling of desperate need and the sense that you have to do something instantly: I must do this right now! This is almost always a sign that identifies an impulse rather than an intuitive feeling. *Intuition* doesn't change over time—you know something is right for you today, and it will be right for you tomorrow, also. With intuition, there is no pressing need to act immediately; you feel as though you can take time to think it over.

Another way to tell the difference between an impulse and intuition is to follow the *Rule of Three*. The first time you get an internal feeling about something, note it and let it go. It could be an impulse, or it could be intuition. Same with the second time you get the feeling; note it and let it go. It could *still* be an impulse rather than intuition at work. But the *third* time you have the feeling, act on it! By this time, an impulse will have died down so any remaining feeling is your intuition.

Think about my impulsive decision to go into business with Winston again. That was a decision made in haste, without listening to my feelings, and based on an immediate sense of urgency. In contrast, when I set up my own practice and went out on my own, I was anxious and concerned, but my intuition told me that the decision was a good one. I was energized and excited by the possibilities and knew that this was a good thing to do. Rather than acting impulsively, I took my time to be sure that the decision would still be right for me. That's the difference in feeling that you get from a decision based on impulse versus intuition.

Impulse	Intuition
Compelling	Consistent
Immediate	Persistent
No time to think	Immediacy is not as important
A feeling of desperate need	Withstands the Law of Three

Your reason and intuition may not always agree. You will have to determine which should govern your decision-making process. Sometimes the logical approach makes more sense, and sometimes your gut will win out and determine the outcome you select. Sometimes you need to tap into your *wisdom*. Wisdom is your guiding sensibility based on your knowledge and on insight gained through your life experience. Together, reason and intuition create wisdom. A wise individual knows that using reason alone shuts him or her off from a rich source of information based on common sense, memories, instinct and inner guidance. Similarly, relying solely on intuition ignores facts and evidence that can improve decision making and ensure the best possible choices. By combining reason and intuition, you are truly well-informed.

> *God,*
> *Grant me the serenity*
> *To accept the things I cannot change,*
> *The courage to change the things I can,*
> *And the wisdom to know the difference.*
> *—Reinhold Niebuhr, The Serenity Prayer*

Remember Crystal? She's the schoolteacher who left her job after 23 years, just before the start of the school year. Crystal's intuition told her that she needed to move on to something else. Her gut feeling was based on her life experience and instinct, and she knew that if she didn't leave, she would be making a mistake. At the same time, Crystal acknowledged the facts. Her job was stable and secure, but she was feeling burned out after 23 years. While losing the income would be a sacrifice, she would have enough to live in relative comfort. When she considered these facts in conjunction with her intuition, Crystal gained certainty that her desire to leave was the right move. She put herself on an upward spiral to success and well-being by engaging her wisdom.

Jane wanted to buy a new car to replace her 9-year-old car, which was no longer reliable. Her intuition told her that now was the right time to buy. She even followed the Rule of Three, and kept coming back to feeling that it was the right time to buy a new car, but the facts told her differently. She was uncertain that she would be receiving a raise this year, and she was still struggling to get out of credit card debt. In the past, Jane would have ignored these facts and gone ahead and purchased a new car. Now, she tapped into her wisdom. Jane recognized that if she purchased a used car at the now low interest rates, she would still be able to meet her financial obligations. She realized that her intuition was telling her to buy a car, not necessarily a new car. Using both reason and intuition helped Jane make a well-informed decision.

Summing Up the Strategy

The POWER Optimist uses all available sources of information when making a decision. This means not only relying on reason and logic, but also using your inner voice to identify the best course of action. By *incorporating intuition with facts when gathering information*, a much richer picture emerges of the situation than when one makes decisions based solely on factual information. For example, suppose you are deciding between two job offers. Even if reason says to take the higher paying job, your intuition may indicate that the less lucrative job is the right one. Your intuition may be telling you that money should not be the definitive factor in making this choice, and you need to pay attention to other criteria.

Along the same lines, being *Well-informed* involves *checking out the facts to help inform your intuitive sense*, instead of basing your actions on intuition alone. Including facts can help clarify your intuition, which is broad-brushed, assesses the big picture and is less concerned with the details. As with Jane, checking out the facts can help you make a better-informed choice while honoring the intent of intuitive information.

Using Both Reason and Intuition means you will be able to *make decisions using wisdom*. Rather than acting on impulse, which is often based on negative patterns, using wisdom entails self-awareness and neutrality. For example, before making any major decisions, stop and ask yourself: Am I acting impulsively? Does my urge to act feel desperate and immediate? Does my decision making feel rushed? Is my need to act based on my negative patterns? If the answer is yes, slow down and tap into your wisdom. Regardless of the situation, when you pay close attention to both factual information and your intuitive senses, you will gain a more complex view of the situation and expand your potential responses. As a result, you are creating conditions for a successful outcome.

GROWING YOUR WELL-INFORMED PRACTICE	
Using Both Reason and Intuition	
Growth Slump	Growth Surge
Make decisions based solely on factual information.	Incorporate intuition with facts when gathering information.
Base actions on intuition alone.	Check out the facts to help inform intuitive sense.
Act on impulse.	Make decisions using wisdom.

TAKING INTENTIONAL RISKS

Creating conditions for success and well-being often necessitates taking risks. By doing things that are new, we expand our perspectives, increase our skills and experience personal growth. In order to do something we've never done before, we have to step outside our *comfort zone* and into our *risk zone.*

Look at the figure above. There are two areas, one nested inside the other. The inner area is the comfort zone. Everyone has one. It's where you feel safe because you are in familiar territory. The larger zone, which surrounds the comfort zone, is your risk zone. This is where you step into the unknown, often feeling some discomfort in the process. The important thing to recognize is that there is no growth inside the comfort zone. There's a lot of safety and familiarity and contentment—but there is no growth. In fact, staying inside your comfort zone for too long puts you in danger of "rust out," a condition of decay due to lack of stimulation and development. To prevent rust out and place yourself on an upward spiral means taking the risk of leaving the safety of your comfort zone.

Life's Risks

To live is to risk dying.
To hope is to risk failure.
But risk must be taken because the greatest hazard in life

is to risk nothing.

If you risk nothing, and do nothing, you dull your spirit.

You may avoid suffering and sorrow, but you cannot learn,

Feel, change, grow, love and live.

Chained by your attitude, you are a slave.

You have forfeited your freedom

Only if you risk, are you free.

—Anonymous

There's no need for you to take uninformed risks—you wouldn't dive into a swimming pool if you weren't absolutely sure that it was filled with water. Life is the same way. The key is to take *intentional* risks—to be in charge of the risk. You decide what the risk will be, when to take it and how much risk you can handle. People's tolerance for exploring new ideas and activities varies widely—some people are perfectly comfortable doing new things and aren't anxious about them. Other people find it difficult to change anything in their lives. Your tolerance level will be different from other people's, so it's important for you to identify your own boundaries. If you want to create conditions for success and achieve your dreams, you need to grow and change. This requires risk, but you are in charge of that risk. That's why it is intentional.

As you move into the risk zone, you will be encountering your *growing edge*. Think about a garden and the new growth that comes with the spring. The area on the shrub that is the new, bright green color of a growth spurt is the plant's growing edge. The trick is to recognize where *your* unique growing edge is—and to step beyond it. Your growing edge tells you how far you want to step into the risk zone. You can put one foot in at a time or leap in with both feet. The choice is yours. You can determine your growing edge by whether the discomfort of growth feels exciting or overwhelming. If you feel energized and stimulated by the risk, you are on the growing edge. If you feel engulfed by anxiety and fear, you are planning on stepping too far into the risk zone. The further inside the risk zone you move, the higher the anxiety and fear will be. The point is to determine for yourself how much discomfort you can tolerate at any given point. Even if growth occurs in very small bursts, you are creating new opportunities for success and fulfillment of your dreams.

One of my clients, Peggy, was thinking about starting her own company. When she initially thought about leaving her job to fly solo, she became paralyzed with indecision and fear, yet she was bored and depressed at the thought of remaining in her current position. When Peggy came to see me, she was stuck. We worked on identifying her growing edge. Peggy began to realize that staying in her current position was not at her growing edge because there were no more challenges to overcome. She needed to take some risks to create an upward spiral of energy and enthusiasm in her life, but she began to recognize that starting her own company was stepping too far into her risk zone. She needed to back up and take a smaller step. Peggy decided to take the intentional risk of working part-time in her current position while gaining the information and skills she would need to be on her own successfully. This plan felt scary and exciting at the same time, so Peggy knew she had correctly identified her growing edge.

> *Nothing is exciting if you know what the outcome is going to be.*
> *—Joseph Campbell*

In order to become an intentional risk-taker, here are some key points to keep in mind.

Don't wait until you are ready. If you've never done something before, whether it's giving a speech, going to a movie alone or buying your first house, it will most definitely cause some anxiety. You don't know what this new thing will be like, whether you'll succeed or even if you'll like it. Normal hesitancy underlies many activities that are new, unusual or different for us, so don't put off taking the risk until you feel ready, because you may never be!

Face your fear. Fear is a natural and healthy part of risk-taking. It lets you know you are stretching your boundaries. To the extent possible, you need to determine whether your fears have any bearing on the risk you are about to take. If your fears are germane to the situation, they need to be considered and dealt with. If, on the other hand, these fears are not relevant to the situation but are born out of anxiety of the unknown, they should not affect your taking the risk. Such fear only prevents you from doing something that would otherwise be valuable and enriching. For example, think about Carol, who is engaged and about to be married. She is understandably anxious and somewhat fearful. If Carol's fear stems from her fiancé's large amount of debt, his inability to communicate about important emotional issues or his abuse of alcohol, it would be germane to her decision about whether or not to get married. But if her fear is simply related to stepping out of her comfort zone and entering this new phase of her life, it shouldn't stop her from getting married.

Gather information. Taking intentional risks means taking the time to find out necessary information. Talk to others who have done what you are setting out to do. Information provides you with a foundation and a safety net as you move into the risk zone. But, you might point out, it's possible to gather information indefinitely and delay taking any kind of risk! How do you know when to stop the preparation process? There's no easy answer and, of course, that point will vary with every different situation. One way to tell that you have gathered enough information and are ready to go ahead and take action is when you no longer feel energized and engaged in the process of information gathering. When you reach this point, it is time to move ahead.

Remind yourself of past successes. Think back to other times when you entered the risk zone and how that felt. For me, buying my house was definitely on my growing edge. I was nervous, of course, but my fears were part of the normal process of moving into my risk zone. I was able to look at my fears and know they were not germane. I had done a lot of research and information gathering, but I was still extremely anxiety-ridden. Then I realized that I had felt the same anxiety about buying my first car. Now, being a car owner is no sweat. This was clear evidence of a simple fact: today's risk zone becomes tomorrow's comfort zone. Remember that endeavors which at first may have seemed risky, or even impossible, are now easy and successful.

Summing Up the Strategy

Taking Intentional Risks means being in charge of when and how you move from your comfort zone into your risk zone. By controlling and planning how you want to *move into your risk zone*, you will avoid stagnating in the comfort zone and missing out on new and interesting experiences. While it is uncomfortable and sometimes anxiety-producing to try new things and place security at stake, this is the only way to grow. Think about asking yourself, "What would I attempt if I knew I would succeed?" Try making a list of some things that seem interesting and which you would do if you had a crystal ball assuring you that everything would go well. This is a great way of preventing rust out and identifying your next arenas for growth and success.

Taking Intentional Risks occurs because you *determine your growing edge*. This is the area far enough outside your comfort zone to cause excitement and a twinge of nervousness but not so far into your risk zone that you become overwhelmed by discomfort and anxiety. I have a friend who is an introvert and very fearful of public speaking. She wants to become more comfortable speaking in front of others. Her growing edge was to join Toastmasters International and to just attend their meetings for three months before even giving any speeches. When I joined Toastmasters, in contrast, my growing edge was giving an icebreaker speech in the first month without notes. The road to success depends on taking risks, but only you can determine your growing edge and the steps that are right for you.

Risk-taking is sometimes viewed as acting recklessly or taking needless chances. *Taking Intentional Risks* is just the opposite. It requires you to *take time for preparation and reflection*. The key to embracing the uncertainty and anxiety that accompany new experiences and change is to gather information and heed relevant fears. Before stepping into your risk zone, think about the following questions: Have I gathered sufficient information to make an informed decision? Are any of my fears relevant to the situation? If so, in what ways do I need to address these fears? By taking the time to prepare and reflect, you will be creating a safety net for yourself as well as ensuring a greater likelihood of success.

GROWING YOUR WELL-INFORMED PRACTICE Taking Intentional Risks	
GROWTH SLUMP	GROWTH SURGE
Stagnate in the comfort zone.	Move into your risk zone.
Become overwhelmed by discomfort and anxiety.	Determine your growing edge.
Act recklessly and take uninformed chances.	Take time for preparation and reflection.

What a sad sight to imagine: the flowers never taking the risk to blossom, fearing exposure to the elements. Life is about taking risks, and it is a risk to grow. We can play it safe and remain curled up like a flower bud, limiting our vulnerability and liability, but this illusion of safety only keeps us dormant. Like the flower that uses the warmth of the sun and the nourishment of the soil to produce its crowning glory, we can rely on our reason and intuition to find our growing edge, to risk opening up, to bloom, letting our beauty and potential dazzle and enrich the world.

Chapter Seven

Evolving—What Can I Learn?

Rehearsing New Life Scripts
Finding Growth-Promoting Insights
Utilizing Self-Acceptance

It turns out that the saying, "You can't teach an old dog new tricks," doesn't apply to humans. Research now reveals that our brains are continuously changing, producing new growth, making new connections. It doesn't matter how old we are, we are still under construction, learning as we go along. One way to learn new tricks is by rehearsing thoughts and behaviors that help us operate in the world more effectively. We are also evolving when we learn from our failures as well as our successes. Successes show us what we are doing correctly. Our failures or mistakes give us important feedback on what we need to change or concentrate on in the future. The most efficient way to learn from our experiences is to practice self-acceptance. Trying to grow and change when we are mired in negativity and self-judgment is like trying to drive with our car's emergency brake on.

My path to creating POWER Optimism was partly laid by failing at a different goal. I intended to start a business where I could help people by applying my unique view of the world. My first venture was as a dating coach. This made perfect sense because I had had a lot of experience dating, and my efforts had clearly been successful since I am now happily married. I thought I could help others accomplish the same in their lives. After several months of advertising and networking, I only received three calls, and none of these individuals was an appropriate candidate for the services I wanted to provide. While being a dating coach didn't work out as a business, I learned a tremendous amount from this "failure." It was as if I were rehearsing for POWER Optimism. The experience showed me what would and wouldn't work in terms of growing a business. It highlighted how I could best use my skills and insights to help people. As a result, I moved on to create POWER Optimism. The fact is, we learn from contrasts. Without the contrast of what doesn't work, it can be hard to tell what *will* work. Without the lack of success and satisfaction I felt as a dating coach, I would not have been able to visualize or create the more fulfilling program and goals of POWER Optimism.

> *Anyone who has never made a mistake has never tried anything new.*
> —*Albert Einstein*

REHEARSING NEW LIFE SCRIPTS

You are the writer, producer, director and star of your own life story—so make sure you have a great script! A life script is more than the words you say or the actions you take. A life script defines the roles you assume in your life. All too often, we were handed negative life scripts in our formative years by parents, relatives, friends, teachers and the culture. We simply continue to play out these roles. Sometimes, we unconsciously create our own life scripts that set the stage for pain and disappointment. To be evolving means to stop enacting negative life scripts and to start utilizing awareness and intention to revise them. Luckily, there are tools that can help us to *Rehearse New Life Scripts*. Some involve rewriting old schemas and replacing negative patterns that may be holding us back. Others focus on creating new story lines and roles in our lives. Here are the tools that can help in writing new life scripts:

Editing Software: Delete the scripts you have that were written using negative filters. These include ineffective schemas and unresolved past events. As you know, these kinds of scripts only lead to unproductive reactions and outcomes. Using editing software to revise your life script lets you decide how you want to interpret your life experience. Remember, your interpretation of an event is more important than the event or situation itself. You can apply the editing software to create a beneficial interpretation, revising your life script in the process.

We all have some parts of our scripts that are outdated. Without editing and revising our scripts, we become like plants in pots that are too small, containers that the plants have outgrown. We need to update our life scripts to foster reaching our full potential in just the same way that a plant needs to be moved to a container that is larger and more appropriate as it grows.

For example, I have an outdated and unproductive life script that says I am not as accomplished as my professional colleagues. In this script, I play the role of an "imposter," just waiting for someone to pronounce me a professional fraud. When I was working to develop a new aspect of my motivational speaking career, I was unconsciously using this imposter script. I had made a video of my work, which I sent to someone who regularly hires speakers for conferences. Along with the video, I asked this man for suggestions about organizations and people to contact about speaking at their events. When the man responded, he made no mention of the video I had provided. My first thought was that he didn't like the video and hadn't mentioned it because he didn't think I was any good. He thought I was an imposter. I knew this kind of thinking was going to take me on a downward spiral, so I decided to edit my imposter script. How else might I explain this situation? It is perfectly plausible that this man was too busy to watch my video; that he watched it but it didn't occur to him to mention it in his email; or that the video didn't have the same meaning for him as it did for me. What is the right answer? I don't know, but I *do* know that updating my outmoded script prevented me from heading on a downward spiral.

Affirmations: Using the present tense, write down positive statements that describe how you want to be. Then, repeat these affirmations to yourself every day. This is an effective technique for developing a totally new script. By repeating the affirmation regularly, you are practicing the new lines and learning the new role. What is the best way to devise an affirmation? The objective is to create an affirmation on your growing edge. An affirmation that is inside your comfort zone is already a part of your life script. Remember, this is about revising your story. An affirmation that is too far beyond your growing edge, that is, too far inside your risk zone, will not be believable to you. You can't rehearse a character that you don't even remotely believe in.

One of my earliest revisions of my life script was the affirmation, "It is safe to risk and be spontaneous." At the time, this was my growing edge because I had adopted a role in life of "playing it safe." I planned everything. I over-studied as a student; I over-prepared as a teacher. I tried to have all the details of a project worked out in advance. As a result, my life lacked the joy of spontaneity and the surprise of the unexpected. Over time, I internalized the affirmation, and it became a part of my new, updated operating system. I was able to create different outcomes based on this new script. For example, I became more imaginative and spontaneous as a teacher, and was eventually asked to be on a committee to develop a new, cutting-edge curriculum, a task that required a high level of creativity and risk-taking. I had grown, so much so that my former affirmation was now a part of my current life script.

Visualization: Create and practice images of what you want to have in your life and how you want your life to be. Mentally practicing something helps get your mind and body ready to achieve it and has been shown to be very effective in sports, the arts and other ventures. Using the brain to visualize an accomplishment helps build both the brain and the muscles required to reach the goal so that one's skills and confidence both improve. In one study, a researcher divided students into three groups: the first group contracted their pinky finger 20 times in a row, twice a week, for a month. The second group visualized moving their finger this way; and the third group didn't do anything. At the end of the month, the first group increased their finger's muscle strength by 33 percent. The third group, which did nothing, saw no increase in their strength. Fascinatingly, the second group, the visualization group, increased their finger strength by 16 percent, even though they hadn't actually moved their fingers in any exercise!

Visualization works because you come to see yourself succeeding and the idea becomes a part of your new life script. At first, the visualization can feel strange or unreal, but soon the new image will grow and it won't feel so far-fetched. You can use visualization to accompany an affirmation or to imagine a successful outcome in a stressful or new circumstance. To use visualization, set aside time several times a week, and think about the outcome you want to accomplish. Think through every step of the process, imagine the muscles or skills you'll use, what you will say and do, and how you feel doing it. Visualize the scene using a slow motion view to really break down the accomplishment. Then, visualize it at regular speed. Use as many of your senses as you can: taste, touch, smell, hearing and sight. Keep visualizing your success and feel the energy of the upward spiral.

Jim Carrey, the famous comedian and actor, says that he became one of the most successful comedians using visualization. When he was just starting out, Carrey used to drive to the Hollywood Hills at night. In his parked car, he'd visualize receiving accolades for his performance in a film and imagine receiving a $10 million check for his work. He thought about how he would feel when he received that $10 million check, acting out the entire scenario in his mind. He even wrote a check to himself for $10 million, which he kept in his wallet! The result? Carrey was eventually paid $10 million for his role in the motion picture, *The Mask*. He then received $20 million for *The Cable Guy*.

I'm not a has-been. I'm a will-be. —Lauren Bacall

Biography: Write about events in your life as if they have already happened, describing the outcomes as you want them to be. By using your biography as a description of what can be possible, it is a powerful tool for uncovering new thoughts, feelings and behaviors you can use to revise your current life script. Your biography can point out possibilities for affirmations and visualizations. Here's one idea to get you started. Pretend you are writing to a very good friend you haven't seen in over a year. Use next year's date and begin with the opening sentence, "This has been a great year." Now describe all the things you have accomplished this year and the things you have learned. Or, you might write an entry in your journal, dating that entry one year in the future. This is an example from my journal, which I wrote on November 21, 2003, when my imposter script started to interfere with writing this book. It is titled "Wildly Successful" and dated November 21, 2004:

> I cannot believe how many people love my book. I am getting rave reviews and the book is selling really well at the seminars and talks I give. I am very proud of the work....
> I am pleased that people really resonate to the message and like the format.... I am working on the audio part of the

program. People have been calling me to book programs and the marketing that I did last year has really paid off. I am getting repeat business and feeling excellent about what I am providing.... With the book finished and the audio well underway, I am free to enjoy the fruits of my labors. I can concentrate on improving my delivery, story telling and acting, and I have really moved to a new plateau.

Obviously, I cannot tell you at this time if what I have written in the journal entry turns out to be true, but I can tell you that predicting these positive outcomes gives me energy and motivation to keep writing this book. By describing my success, I am now ready to live it!

Act "As If": Decide on a role and then think and behave as if this script is a current reality. Research on cognitive-behavior therapy has shown that our thoughts, feelings and actions are changed when we act "as if" something is already true. The expression, *Fake it 'til you make it*, speaks to the same idea. If you act like something is true, you can begin to experience a physical shift in your energy. Actors experience this shift of energy during the rehearsal process. By trying out new actions or focusing on a particular inner thought, the actor is creating the character. You can do the same thing when you act "as if." Sit, walk or talk as the "old you," the role you want to revise. Notice the ways you feel limited, constricted or restrained. Now, rehearse a new script. Sit, walk and talk in your new role. Notice how your energy changes as you create a script that allows you to feel open, empowered and energized.

> *Life can only be understood backwards,*
> *but it must be lived forwards.* —Soren Kirekegaard

I knew I needed to revise an outmoded life script in my personal life when it came to dating. I had adopted a "victim role," choosing men who were unavailable. Of course, the scenes with men ended with me feeling abandoned, unattractive and hopeless. I decided it was time to rehearse a new role. I was going to act as if I were a goddess. I practiced walking like a goddess, sitting like a goddess and visualized new scenes in my head. One Saturday night I went out on a date with a man named Bob. It was our sixth date, and it was a couple of weeks before the Fourth of July. I brought up planning something for the Fourth, but Bob had a ton of reasons why we couldn't get together for that day. Immediately, my victim role kicked in. "Of course he doesn't want to spend the Fourth with me," I thought. "I'm uninteresting, unattractive, boring." But something different happened. I decided, right then and there, that I was going to act like a goddess. In this new role, I had to figure out what a goddess would say and do. A goddess wouldn't sulk or try to wheedle Bob into making a date with her. As a goddess, I simply said, "OK, never mind. I'll find someone else to go out with on the Fourth." Equally important, I made a mental note to myself not to go out with Bob anymore.

The next day, Sunday, I had a blind date. We went to brunch and then for a walk, and I was in my goddess energy. We had a great time. On Monday, he called me up and said, "You strike me as the kind of woman who is going to have a lot of offers for the Fourth of July. So, even though it's still a couple of weeks away, and we only just met, would you go out with me on the Fourth?" Of course, I said yes, thinking to myself, "This goddess stuff really works!" Two weeks later we went out on the Fourth—and two years later, Jules and I got married.

We create the scenes in our lives by the scripts we adopt and the roles we choose to play. Did my deciding to act like a goddess *guarantee* that I would meet someone to spend the holiday with? Guarantee that Jules and I would get along so well we'd get married? No. Of course not. But what it *did* do was shift my thinking about dating men like Bob, who weren't really interested in a long-term relationship. It also enabled me to create an openness to the possibility of being with someone like Jules. Rehearsing my life script as a goddess helped me to visualize having that life and to experience the exuberance that being a goddess entails. Once you act as if you have a new script, you can start to see it as possible and begin to make it happen in your life.

> *To exist is to change, to change is to mature, to mature is to go on creating oneself endlessly.*
> —Henri Bergson

Summing Up the Strategy

Rehearsing New Life Scripts means thinking about your life story as something that can be changed and improved. You can *identify and delete obsolete scripts*, thereby eliminating roles that are no longer useful or productive. Keeping scripts that were written long ago and contain negative schemas and self-perceptions impedes your ability to create a life that will bring you success. If you fail to recognize life scripts that are outdated and obsolete, you run the risk of staying stuck in a rut and not living up to your own potential for happiness. If I had kept the script that put me in an imposter role, I would never have gained the confidence I needed to develop a business, speak professionally or write this book. If you are not creating the success and enjoyment you desire in your life, determine what script may be holding you back and make a personal commitment to erase it.

A new life script won't just appear out of the blue. It has to be nourished and created. As you move to change the way you see your life potential, you will need to *develop new scripts by using affirmations, visualization and biography.* With these techniques, you can imagine yourself successfully accomplishing something that may once have seemed far-fetched. Suppose you were told as a child that you were not smart enough to graduate from college. This is your life script. You can develop a new role by creating the growing edge affirmation, "I pass my college courses." Visualize yourself sitting in class, answering questions, participating in discussions, doing library research, getting back your tests and receiving passing grades. Now write your biography as if you were a college graduate. Once you practice something in your head, it becomes much easier to achieve it in real life.

Rehearsing New Life Scripts involves expanding the roles you play by acting "as if." In this way, you begin to integrate the new thoughts, feelings and behaviors you were at first imagining into your actual behavior. By practicing a new role, you bring a new sense of yourself into the world. Without this rehearsal, you limit your repertoire of roles. One of the key principles of changing your old life script is to deliberately rehearse the new script. For example, if you want to develop a role of self-confidence, practice moving, sitting, breathing and gesturing as if you were confident. Wear new clothes, cologne, jewelry or accessories that say "confident." Eat a meal as a confident person would. At first, you may feel artificial. With practice, however, you will be integrating your new role into your life, and it will become a natural part of your self.

GROWING YOUR EVOLVING PRACTICE Rehearsing New Life Scripts	
GROWTH SLUMP	GROWTH SURGE
Fail to recognize outdated scripts.	Identify and delete obsolete scripts.
Maintain old scripts by default.	Develop new scripts by using affirmations, visualization and biography.
Limit your role repertoire.	Expand the roles you play by acting "as if."

FINDING GROWTH-PROMOTING INSIGHTS

All of life's lessons offer the opportunity for growth. Remember, as human beings we are continually "under construction," developing ourselves and improving. Because we are *Evolving*, we will always make mistakes. Growth comes from mistakes—from trying, and failing, and then trying again. In order to turn mistakes into learning, you must practice *Finding Growth-Promoting Insights*. When you make a mistake, you can spiral downward, give up in frustration and stop trying new things. By finding the lesson in the mistake, by identifying what you can learn from the failure, you are creating insights that will help you grow, placing you on an upward spiral and keeping you motivated to keep trying. By *Finding Growth-Promoting Insights*, you are learning from your experiences in ways that expand your horizons and abilities.

> *Life is like playing a violin and learning the instrument*
> *at the same time.*
> —George Eliot

In reality, all experiences are lessons, of whether they are successes or failures. A successful outcome lets you know you are on course and reinforces your thoughts, feelings and behaviors. Mistakes, on the other hand, let you know that adjustments need to be made. Insights from your failed experiences are as much a part of your growth and development as the experiences that work. In fact, if you only experienced success, you would stop growing. Why is this? Because we learn from trial-and-error and from contrast. In other words, we learn by comparing what works to what doesn't work. If we never failed, we would have no point of reference for comparison. Another way to think about this concept is that when we succeed, we learn one possible path for a positive outcome. We can continue to move along this path, but eventually, we will become bored and the path will turn into a rut. When we fail, we are forced to explore new options, to figure out what went wrong and discover new possibilities for success. In this way, we find ourselves on new trails, looking at new scenery. Our mistakes and failures force us to consider different paths in life.

Here are a few short vignettes to illustrate the power of growth-promoting insights:[1]

- Bill Walton is one of the greatest centers in basketball history. He is now an extremely successful basketball broadcaster. Yet Walton suffered from a severe speech impediment—he stuttered until he was 28 years old. In fact, he stuttered so badly he would dread talking to the media after games at UCLA. Today, he attributes a measure of his success to all the failure and embarrassment he had to overcome, explaining he is a better and happier person because of his struggles.

- Post-It® Notes is one of the best selling products of the 3M Company, yet it got its start with a failure. A scientist at 3M was working to improve the glue on Scotch tape. The new formula he devised would stick at first, but then was easily pulled off. By accident, another man in the company, Art Fry, recognized the value of the formula. With this insight, he started trying the glue in different ways and finally came up with the Post-It® Note, turning a mistake into a success.

- John Irving is an accomplished novelist, having written over a dozen novels. While he has had two of his novels made into movies, when it came time to transfer the book *Cider House Rules* from the page to the screen, Irving wanted to write the screenplay himself. He states that "the most radical decisions of what not to use in the novel, I made those decisions in the first draft of the screenplay." Nevertheless, it took him repeated rewrites to get the screenplay right. This is the purpose of contrast, discovering what will work by learning from what doesn't work. Earlier versions of the screenplay were too bleak, and Irving and the director worked together to create a version that would keep central relationships between characters in proper balance to the film as a whole. In fact, there were about 50 drafts of the screenplay.

- Harrison Ford is a superstar, with a career spanning over 25 years. Yet, when Ford tried to break into the movie world as an actor in the Sixties, he was unsuccessful. He turned to carpentry instead, fine-tuning this craft, and soon found himself as a carpenter to the stars, earning a top reputation for his woodwork skills. As Ford sees it, his skills as a carpenter paid off in providing him with the processes and perspective he uses to develop his characters, such as having a logical plan, perceiving the project from the ground up and laying a firm foundation. Rather than viewing his years as a carpenter as a failure, Ford recognizes that the insights from this craft have supported his success as an actor.

What do these stories tell us about *Finding Growth-Promoting Insights*? A failure is only a failure if we don't learn anything from it. By finding the lesson, we can let go of the emotion and disappointment that accompanies mistakes and lack of success, get up and try again. The insight is the catalyst we need to create opportunities for growth and success.

Remember the story I told earlier about how I had picked up my rock of limiting beliefs while I was at a mentoring camp for youth? I came home from that experience depressed about my qualities as a mentor, a swirl of negative emotions. I did not take the time to deal with these feelings but instead got right back into the swing of things and began doing errands. I parallel parked my car on the street and went to the bank and post office. When I returned to my car, someone else had parked in front of me, and the space was now really tight. To get out I had to go backward and forward several times, and in doing so, I tapped the car in back of me, just a little tap. I turned around to face front, and there was a man standing in front of my car, screaming at me, "You damaged my car. You broke my transmission and now you're fleeing the scene of a crime!" The man was completely incensed and out of control, so I decided to call the police, who filled out an accident report. By the time I got home, I was a real mess. I felt like a failed mentor, a bad driver and a flawed human being.

After I calmed down, I reflected on the incident and was able to gain some insight. I learned several important lessons from that experience. The first lesson: I will always make mistakes. In fact, that's why cars have bumpers—in recognition of the fact that no one can drive through life without making some mistakes along the way. The second lesson: I need to practice what I preach. I knew I was dragging around my rock, but I still went off in a big flurry of negativity and activity. I ignored my own wisdom and made my problems worse. I learned, once again, the value of sitting down quietly, identifying my limiting beliefs, dropping my rock and regulating my emotions. It seems that a lesson is repeated until it is learned. The third lesson: It's important to keep things in perspective and keep a sense of humor. That man yelling at me that I had broken his transmission by tapping his car was outrageous, but it wasn't any more outrageous than my telling myself that I was a failure as a mentor. I have named the angry man "Transmission Man," and when I recall how he overreacted to the littlest tap on his car, I actually start to laugh at him. Remembering the incident helps me to see that I am acting just like Transmission Man when I hold onto my negative and limiting beliefs, which are so outrageous they are actually funny. Transmission Man helps me laugh at myself whenever I fall prey to my own limiting beliefs.

> *We tend to listen to the shouts that are outside of us*
> *rather than the small voices inside of us, and when we do that,*
> *we deny ourselves opportunity.* —Steven Spielberg

No one has a smooth path in life. Everyone—everyone—has ups and downs, successes and failures. People who seem the most successful will often talk about how much they had to struggle and learn as they worked to achieve their goals. In fact, progress and success are not achieved in a straight line, but in a series of loops. From time to time, we experience ourselves regressing, looping down. It's the familiar statement, "Two steps forward and one step back," in action. But why is this necessary? In reality, the loop back represents the lesson we need to learn in order to reach our next plateau. What we gain from our insight gives us the energy and the momentum to move forward to the next level.

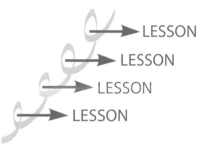

LESSON

LESSON

LESSON

LESSON

The next time you make a mistake, experience a failure or regress in your thoughts, feelings or behaviors, don't beat yourself up about it. Don't keep going over and over the mistake or failure in your head or dwelling on the disappointment. Instead, ask yourself, "What can I learn here? What is an insight that will help me grow?" Appreciate the insight and learn from it and let go of the feelings. The purpose of the feelings is to get you to focus on the lesson. Once you have learned the lesson, you are ready to let go of the mistake and move on.

Remember Jane from the opening chapter of the book, who took my class when she was going through a divorce and feeling really depressed and anxious? For her, *Finding Growth-Promoting Insights* has been particularly useful. Here's what she says about it: "Learning from a 'bad' situation allows me to move on and lets me reach closure. For example, this really helped me learn from my experience going through a divorce. It helped me to discover why the marriage didn't work, and what lessons I could learn from that. I discovered that my own negative feelings about life in general had shaped my views about relationships and particularly marriage. I thought marriage had to be perfect all the time. If it wasn't perfect, the marriage had to be flawed. Of course, nothing is perfect all of the time—I know that now. Since the marriage wasn't perfect, I became extremely negative about it and very controlling towards my husband. I've learned that those traits contributed to the downfall of my marriage. I think self-awareness is the key to change. As I worked on *Evolving*, I became much more aware of my own negativity. Realizing the truth about my negativity opened the door for me to alter my perceptions, to change my interpretations and ultimately to be more positive towards myself and others. I've taken what I learned into my new relationship: I don't expect things to be perfect all the time, and I'm no longer controlling. I simply focus on the good points and enjoy life."

Summing Up the Strategy

Finding Growth-Promoting Insights is a reality-based strategy that *recognizes that growth comes from failure as well as success.* Instead of assigning a negative connotation to mistakes and failures, use them as ways to grow and learn. Take the lesson from the experience and apply it to the future so that you will be stronger, more focused and better prepared for whatever comes your way. Remember, no actor is going to get every part he auditions for. No politician will win every race. Not everyone you ask on a date is going to be interested in going out with you. You won't get every job you apply for. You may get a speeding ticket, forget to send an important email or ruin the meal for Thanksgiving. The important factor is that each failed situation in your life brings the opportunity to learn more about yourself. Use this knowledge to grow and expand.

The POWER Optimist *appreciates the insight and lets go of the mistake or disappointment.* For example, I was initially very upset by Transmission Man's yelling at me about my driving, but once I gained insight from the event, it was time to let go of the mistake. I learned what I needed from the experience, and it was also time to let go of any negative feelings of disappointment or anger I had towards myself. After all, I had learned quite a bit about myself and life from Transmission Man. My mistakes reminded me of adjustments I needed to make. You can't learn and grow if you are continually beating yourself up about what's gone wrong or how you failed. If you focus on mistakes or disappointments and continue to experience the negative feelings, you lose the opportunity to make changes and enhance your life, and you are forgetting that growth comes from trial-and-error, from the very act of making mistakes and being disappointed.

Finally, *Finding Growth-Promoting Insights* means *recognizing that progress is a process of downturns and upturns*. Be realistic and open-minded about the process of growth. Believing that progress occurs in a straight line is an unrealistic expectation. Remember, one success does not mean that you will never have any problems again. In fact, relying too much on past success is a sure way to lose your growing edge and to risk stagnation. Nor does one failure spell doom for any accomplishments on your part. When you have a disappointment, don't give up. Learn from it. Both the ups and downs are necessary for you to grow and create conditions for success in your life. For example, when you have a success—study it. Learn why you achieved your goal, understand what worked so you can build on it and recognize your role so you can repeat it. When you have a failure—learn from it. Do something differently next time, activate new thoughts and behaviors and remind yourself that you are never too old to learn and grow. There is no part of life that does not contain lessons. If you are alive, there are downturns and upturns to be experienced.

GROWING YOUR EVOLVING PRACTICE	
Finding Growth-Promoting Insights	
GROWTH SLUMP	**GROWTH SURGE**
Assign a negative connotation to mistakes and failures.	Recognize that growth comes from failure as well as success.
Focus on mistakes or disappointments and continue to experience the negative feelings.	Appreciate the insight and let go of the mistake or disappointment.
Believe progress is made in a straight line.	Recognize that progress is a process of downturns and upturns.

UTILIZING SELF-ACCEPTANCE

Since we humans are always under construction, what is the best way to facilitate changes and motivate ourselves for continued growth? There are two possibilities. You can use the lens of judgment, and look at yourself and your life negatively, making changes because of self-blame and guilt, or you can *Utilize Self-Acceptance*, assessing yourself and your life neutrally in order to figure out what you can learn and do differently in the future.

Utilizing Self-Acceptance means silencing the *critic* that lives within you, listening instead to your inner *mentor*, the voice representing your inner sense of self validation. The critic says, "You did something wrong, so change it." That's operating from a position of blame and opens you up to feelings of worthlessness. It implies that you have not measured up in some way. The critic gears up your negative tapes, schemas and patterns. The mentor, alternatively, asks, "What can I do in the future to improve on this outcome?" This question implies that you are always growing and learning. In fact, even if you assess a situation as "a job well-done," the question of improvement is still valid because there are always possibilities for new options and choices.

While both the critic and the mentor have the same purpose—to produce learning and growth—the mentor's question is a positive one that facilitates the change process. Here's why: compare *self-acceptance* to *self-criticism*, and think about the feelings each generates. Self-acceptance facilitates growth and change by increasing energy, affirmation, openness, creativity, positive visions, inspiration, new possibilities and motivation. Self-acceptance generates an upward spiral of growth that leads to greater success and well-being. On the other hand, self-criticism stunts growth and change by sapping energy, denying praise, closing the self off from others, limiting creativity, hampering one with negative beliefs and thoughts and closing off motivation and energy. When the critic is stronger than the mentor, you will move along a downward spiral. If, on the other hand, the mentor is stronger, you will move along an upward spiral.

Let me give you an example from my life concerning my desire to eat in a healthier manner. As I mentioned earlier, I have done a lot of work on improving my body image. However, I still experience self-criticism about my body from time to time, especially after seeing one too many advertisements about losing weight. At these moments, when I am judging myself negatively, I am hoping that I will be motivated to eat better, but what ends up happening is I become dissatisfied with myself and my body. This fuels negative feelings, which leads to increased eating as I turn to food to comfort myself from negative feelings. As a result of listening to my inner critic, I have placed myself on a definite downward spiral, sapped my energy and increased my overeating (particularly of junk food). On the other hand, when I listen to my inner mentor, I am *more likely* to eat well and improve my health. My mentor encourages me to accept my body while I acknowledge that there is room for improvement in my eating habits. The better I feel about my body, the better I eat. After all, why would I abuse something I like? I don't feel bad about myself. I don't need comfort from food. I am not at war with my body, so I am not moving on a downward spiral. I know that I don't have to lose a certain amount of weight to be OK; I am OK already! In this way, I gain energy from accepting where I am now, and then I use that energy to make improvements in my eating choices and exercise routine.

The mentor speaks from a position of *continuing excellence*. From this perspective, you know you have done the best you can at any given moment. You also acknowledge the next moment brings new opportunities for more excellence, learning and growth. The critic often speaks from a position of *perfectionism*. From this point of view, you expect yourself to have already accomplished the ideal or perfect outcome. If you perceive an outcome as less than perfect, you become overwhelmed or paralyzed by thoughts of inferiority, inadequacy and deficiency. You also become worried and anxious about making another mistake. You struggle with fear and doubt, making it extremely hard to let go of what you have done and move on to the next moment.

I think rehearsal is a necessity.
You have to be able to fail
in order to succeed.
—Joanne Woodward

Imagine you are an actor watching your performance in a movie. Think about how you would feel if your thoughts were based on continuing excellence. You might say to yourself, "That scene didn't go the way I thought it would. I did the best I could, but perhaps if I make a different choice in the way I say that line or in my objective in the scene, it will go better. I'll remember these options and try them in the next take." Continuing excellence leads to acceptance because you know you can always improve. Contrast the way that feels with thoughts based on perfectionism, such as "That scene didn't go the way I thought it would. I should have made a different choice. I can't believe I did it this way. I should have done better." The belief in the possibility of perfection leads to self-criticism because you have unrealistic expectations of yourself. By practicing self-acceptance and continuing excellence, you can walk away with a sense of satisfaction even if you need to redo the scene. By falling into the trap of idealism, you run the risk of constant dissatisfaction because you can never really be perfect.

Utilizing Self-Acceptance involves moving past two prevalent myths about acceptance that can hold you back.[2] The first myth confuses acceptance with approval. It is the false notion that accepting something about yourself or your life means you approve of it. In fact, you can accept a current situation without necessarily *liking* it. For example, one of my clients, Judith, is married to an alcoholic. When she came to see me, Judith had been trying to get her husband to stop drinking, but to no avail. Her inner critic was sitting on her shoulder scolding her for failing to stop her husband's alcohol abuse. Judith needed to accept that her husband's addiction was his problem, not hers. Alcoholism is a disease, and an alcoholic needs to seek help for him or herself. Judith worked on accepting the situation. She didn't like the fact that her husband was still drinking, but she was eventually able to accept the fact that his drinking had nothing to do with her. She stopped criticizing herself for his addiction and accepted that she couldn't cure or control his alcoholism. She experienced a greater sense of well-being as a result of her acceptance of the problem, even though she still did not approve of her husband's behavior.

The second myth about self-acceptance concerns change and is the mistaken notion that if you accept who and what you are, you will be indifferent to change. In fact, the opposite is true. If you can accept yourself, you can take charge of creating change and growth. You don't have to deny your weaknesses or hide your desires for fear of appearing "bad," "not good enough" or "incompetent." Self-acceptance allows you to neutrally assess what is true for you in the current moment. Loving and accepting yourself *as you are* does not mean that you want to *keep* everything about yourself the same. It doesn't mean that you can't change or wouldn't be more fulfilled if you worked on certain things about yourself or your life. You just love yourself and accept yourself as you are right now, *and* you want to keep growing and evolving.

Summing Up the Strategy

One of the key strategies for *Utilizing Self-Acceptance* is to *listen to your mentor to motivate and facilitate changes* in your self or life. Too often, however, we beat ourselves up about our own shortcomings. This is giving power to the voice of the inner critic that harangues us about our lack of success and for whom nothing is ever good enough. The critical voice is deflating and places you on a downward spiral. In contrast, the voice of your mentor is energizing and places you on an upward spiral by noting that more is always possible. Think about a situation that you want to change and improve in your life. Invite your mentor to come forward. You will know you are listening to your mentor when you hear a voice that speaks to you with words of validation, helps you make positive changes in your life by cheering you on and encourages you to reach for new accomplishments. The feedback you give yourself as your own mentor can help you grow, learn and evolve to create greater conditions for success.

The POWER Optimist *embraces an attitude of continuing excellence.* This is the view that even as we do our best, there are always new possibilities for growth. There is no point where you stop learning or growing in your life. This is one of the wonderful things about being human. By focusing on continuing excellence, you give up on the notion of perfectionism. Perfectionism is a manifestation of fear and self-criticism growing from a sense that your accomplishments will never be good enough. It blocks you from starting new or creative ventures since your critic knows no accomplishment will ever pass muster. In contrast, when you adopt an attitude of continuing excellence, your life becomes a glorious adventure. What a relief to be able to be "good enough," to know that you are doing your best at any given moment and to look forward to gains and improvements in your life. Let yourself relax. Lighten up. Enjoy the journey and watch yourself evolve through the lens of validation and self-acceptance.

Finally, *Utilizing Self-Acceptance* involves accurately assessing yourself and your life. Remember, it is not realistic to pretend that you like and approve of everything about yourself and your life. Nor is it realistic to deny the aspects of yourself or your life that are not working for you. Instead, ask yourself: How would I describe myself and my life right now? What are my strengths and weaknesses at this time? What do I want, need, think, feel at the present moment? By neutrally observing your own life, you will be able to see what you would like to change or where you could be more satisfied. By not denying your reality, but rather accepting yourself and your life as it is in the present moment, you will truly be able to identify what is working and what needs attention and to honestly set about creating conditions for success that will place you on an upward spiral.

GROWING YOUR EVOLVING PRACTICE Utilizing Self-Acceptance	
GROWTH SLUMP	GROWTH SURGE
Listen to your critic when trying to make changes.	Listen to your mentor in order to motivate and facilitate changes.
Adopt an attitude of perfectionism.	Embrace an attitude of continuing excellence.
Deny your current reality.	Accurately assess yourself and your life.

As plants mature, the landscape of the garden evolves and changes. As we ripen with age, the landscape of our lives can take on new shapes and opportunities. We rehearse new possibilities, learn new facets of ourselves, develop insights that help us unleash our potential and harness our energy for continued growth. Along the way, our paths will be strewn with the remains of our failures. We can look at each of these mishaps not with fear or blame or shame, but rather with appreciation, for they represent the lessons we learn along life's journey.

Chapter Eight

Resilient—What is a Motivating Interpretation?

Adopting a Positive Outlook
Regulating Emotion
Finding Meaning in Adversity

A part of life is facing the unexpected difficulties, losses and traumas that inevitably arise. Life is filled with stressors that result in our feeling angry and frustrated, and life sometimes hands us tragedies that leave us miserable, depressed and grief-stricken. When you feel as if the rug has been pulled out from under you or when your internal rubber band has been stretched to the max, resiliency comes into play. Resiliency refers to a person's capacity to recover from negative events. It is the ability to spring back and rebound despite the stress of today's world. It is the capacity to successfully adapt to adversity. Being optimistic is not about trying to pretend bad things won't happen—or ignoring them when they do. Instead, optimism is about finding a way to go on. By identifying a motivating interpretation, you gain the energy you need to move forward when confronted with distress and hardship.

One of the widows in my dissertation study illustrates what it means to be *Resilient* in the way she coped with the death of her husband of 45 years. She was able to grieve for her loss while demonstrating resiliency at the same time. She kept a journal and discovered, as she periodically read earlier entries, tangible evidence that she was improving. This enabled her to tap into hopefulness and feel a sense of openness compared to the closeness that accompanied her earlier sorrow. She was able to adopt an attitude of possibility by reminding herself that things will never be the same, but she would someday feel happy again. When her grief felt overwhelming, especially as her wedding anniversary approached, she decided to try a diversion and took a trip to visit a good friend. As time progressed, she was able to recognize that she had actually experienced changes in her self-concept. She took control of her finances and even got a part-time job. As a result of these new endeavors, she felt more confident and independent and was even contemplating taking a cruise by herself.

Resiliency is not a new concept. Researchers began to explore resiliency in 1955 by tracking over 500 children in Hawaii who were born into poverty. Some faced additional problems that placed them at high risk, such as having their family break up, having an alcoholic or mentally ill family member or seeing a family member die. All of the children were followed from birth until age 30. Despite the challenges and hardships they faced, scientists found that as early as age 18, one-third of the high risk group had managed to overcome these hurdles. By age 30, over 80% of the larger group was thriving. Intrigued, researchers wanted to know how so many of these children managed to fare so well. Using data from this and other studies, scientists have reported two major findings concerning resiliency. First, we all have some capacity for resiliency. Resiliency is innate. And second, they concluded that resiliency can also be taught. We can boost our capacity to contend with the stresses and losses we encounter by learning how to be more resilient.[1]

The strategies in the *Resilient* practice are designed to increase your capacity to bounce back. By learning to adopt a positive attitude and manage your emotions effectively, you are creating a protective cushion from the stresses and frustrations of your life. By finding meaning when adversity strikes, you can move more readily from loss to recovery to positive growth.

ADOPTING A POSITIVE OUTLOOK

Adopting a Positive Outlook is not a matter of hiding your head in the sand and pretending everything is OK when it might not be. It means, instead, practicing behaviors that help you reach a motivating interpretation of your difficult experiences rather than being defeated by them. In this section, I'll talk about several strategies for adopting a positive outlook. Not only do these strategies help you to react in a resilient manner to the specific stresses of your everyday life, but they also build resiliency over time. By using these strategies consistently, you can build up a cushion of resiliency that will buffer you when disappointments or frustrations come up.

Adopt a positive explanatory style. By "explanatory style," I mean the way you interpret what is happening around you and to you. What do you say to yourself to explain a success or a disappointment in your life? Research shows that a person's explanatory style is different depending on whether she is an optimist or a pessimist. Let's look at how this would play out in someone's life. Joey and Suzy both just took a test at school and scored really well on it. Joey is an optimist; research shows that this means he looks at success as permanent, pervasive and personal. Because he thinks that success is permanent, Joey says to himself, "I did well on this test, and I'll do well on the next one." Optimists see success as something that will re-occur. Also, because he believes that success is pervasive, Joey thinks, "I did well on this test, and I'll do well on a test in another subject, too." Optimists see success as something that exists in more than one area. Finally, because he thinks that success is personal, Joey reasons, "I studied hard; I am the reason I did well on the test." Optimists see success as something that they caused.

Optimists see success as permanent, pervasive and personal.
Pessimists see success as temporary, specific and impersonal.

Now, let's look at Suzy, who is a pessimist. Not surprisingly, research shows that pessimists see things differently. For them, success is temporary, specific and impersonal. Suzy thinks, "I did well on that test, but I won't be able to do well the next time." Success is temporary; it doesn't last. Suzy also says to herself, "Well, I did fine on that test, but it must have been a really easy exam." Because she sees success as specific, she feels that it only applies to that one, particular experience. Finally, Suzy thinks, "Anybody could have done well on that test." Because success is viewed as impersonal, success does not necessarily imply anything about the pessimist's abilities. It's the way you interpret the events—your explanatory style—that determines the meaning you assign to what happens to you. This goes back to what we were talking about in the very beginning, that your interpretation of the event is more important than the event itself. It's important to work to create interpretations that are permanent, pervasive and personal. When something good happens, take credit for your successes, praise yourself and remember that you made it happen.

One of my clients, Jennifer, was a teacher whose students were adults working toward their General Equivalency Diploma (GED). She got great evaluations from her students but was completely insecure about her abilities. She was always afraid that her next class would be terrible and that she would do poorly the next time her boss came in to observe a class. She was always waiting for a crisis to occur and for the proverbial "other shoe" to drop. For Jennifer, her abilities in the classroom were flukes and short-term events; her success was temporary. She didn't interpret her popularity with her students as saying anything about her abilities. Her popularity was impersonal, and she felt that just because one class had gone well didn't mean that the next session would be a success—the success was specific. You can see, Jennifer had a pessimistic explanatory style.

Jennifer and I worked on creating new interpretations that were based on optimism and a positive explanatory style. Jennifer had to learn to change her thoughts and her behaviors so that her feelings about her abilities would change, too. So, Jennifer started adopting a positive outlook and explanatory style. When her class went well, she said to herself, "I did well in this class, and I'll do well with the next. I did well with this subject, so I'll do well with another subject. I am a successful teacher due to my skills, intuition and experience." When she dealt well with a disciplinary problem, she said, "I can handle difficult students not just due to luck but also because of my wisdom and personal experience in the classroom." Her interpretation (and hence her feeling) became: "I was a success at this, and I'll be good at it the next time, too."

Over time, Jennifer's reality shifted so that this positive interpretation became the underlying tape for her life. Eventually, it began to reflect her feelings about herself. She learned to affirm her accomplishments and believe that her talents were permanent and an intrinsic part of her personality. She recognized that her abilities in one area carried over to other areas as well; they were pervasive. Finally, Jennifer recognized her skills were personal; they were not externally created, but something intrinsic to her self.

Optimists explain their disappointments as temporary, specific, not entirely personal.

What happens when optimists experience setbacks, glitches or false starts? Interestingly, optimists explain non-success in much the same way as pessimists explain success. In other words, optimists view non-success as temporary, specific and not entirely personal. If something doesn't work out, it is short-term, pertains to one event only and is not due solely to personal attributes or abilities. Here are some examples of individuals who were not stopped by roadblocks or rejections on their way to success:

- Babe Ruth struck out 1,330 times on his way to the Baseball Hall of Fame.

- Elvis Presley was banished from the Grand Ole Opry after one performance and was told, "You ain't going nowhere, son."

- Oprah Winfrey was fired from her television reporter job and was told, "You're not fit for TV."

It is unlikely that any of these individuals would have reached their potential had they interpreted these setbacks as permanent, pervasive or personal.[2]

Think back to Chapter Two and the illusions that contain two images. Using a positive explanatory style is choosing the image that puts you on an upward spiral. It involves eliminating the negative pattern of interpretation and establishing a new pathway that is more positive. Switching from a pessimistic to a positive explanatory style can take a lot of reminding, reinforcement and affirmations. When things go well, you have to keep reassuring yourself that the success will continue and is a result of your abilities. When things don't go well, remember that these setbacks are only a temporary glitch due to specific circumstances.

Practice appreciation. Sometimes in the rush of everyday life, we tend to focus on the things that are not going right rather than notice the many positive things that surround us. Concentrating on the negatives creates a downward spiral and can increase frustration and worry. Focusing on the good things in life can help reinforce an upward spiral. This provides a buffer when stressful events occur by placing things in context and reinforcing the fact that nothing is all bad. There is good that occurs in everyone's life. The trick is to pay attention and take notice. Here are some ways to increase your appreciation for the good things in life.

- **Say "thank you" for the little things.** By saying "thank you" for the everyday, ordinary, positive events that occur, you become aware of how much good there is in your life. These events can be a convenient parking space in your neighborhood, a nice conversation with a family member, a walk through the autumn leaves, a great day at work, a delicious apple or a fun new purchase. The more you practice thankfulness, the happier you become because you are establishing a pattern of noticing good things in your life. Try saying "thank you" out loud. This helps reinforce your awareness and bolsters your positive attitude and feelings.

  Saying "thank you" also involves accepting compliments you receive. Think about a time when someone paid you a compliment, and you responded reflexively by discounting the praise and explaining it away. ("The project wasn't really that hard," or "You're just being nice," are two examples.) This kind of response, while it may seem modest, actually negates your accomplishments and downplays your successes. It also devalues the other person's opinion! Instead of deflecting the compliment, smile and say, "Thanks!" or, "Yes, I'm really proud of how that went." You not only honor the other person by recognizing the compliment he or she gave you but also accept value for your own achievement.

- **Observe nature with appreciation.** One very easy way to generate appreciation is to spend more time with nature. Immersing yourself in nature, either deeply or fleetingly, can help even the most harried person create a sense of calm. Go for a walk at a nearby park, community garden or nature trail. Go looking specifically for something beautiful, such as a colorful bird or flower, and give yourself a break from your own emotions and thoughts, or you can just be in nature without a purpose and appreciate what is around you in the moment. You'll find that your emotions are softened and your feelings soothed by being outside and away from your normal environment. Every season carries its own unique form of beauty. There is nothing quite like the view of snow right after it's fallen, colorful autumn leaves, a crisp spring morning or sunshine on a summer day. Whatever time of year it is, and wherever you live, get outside yourself by getting outside into nature.

- *Keep a gratitude log.* One easy and helpful way to practice appreciation is to actively note the things for which you are thankful. Many people keep a record, called a "gratitude log," of the good things that happen to them and make them appreciative. A gratitude log is merely a list of things you feel grateful or thankful for. Some people keep a special notebook for their gratitude list and write down 10 things that they are grateful for every night before they go to sleep or every morning when they get up. Your list might include a great lunch, the fact that your cat curled up with you while you were reading the paper, good feedback you received at work, a beautiful sunset or hearing your favorite song on the radio. You might also want to include people who have influenced your life in positive and supportive ways.

It now appears that, over time, people who keep a gratitude journal become more appreciative in general, which leads them to greater optimism and happiness with their lives. A recent study compared three groups: one whose members kept a gratitude log, a second whose members listed complaints they had about their day and a third who listed ways they were better off than others. After three weeks, the gratitude log group reported that they felt better and more joyful, had more energy, had fewer complaints about their health and felt more life satisfaction than those in the other two groups. Participants also said that the longer they kept their gratitude journal, the easier it became to think of things to put on their lists. Looking for good things made it easier for people to find the good things in their lives. The research on gratitude logs indicates that people can learn how to tweak their attitudes and increase their positive coping skills which maximizes their ability to see things optimistically.[3]

> *Write the wrongs that are done to you in the sand,*
> *but write the good things that happen to you in marble.*
> *Let go of all emotions such as resentment and retaliation,*
> *which diminish you. Hold onto the emotions,*
> *such as gratitude and joy, which enrich you.*
> *—Arab proverb*

Reframe the event. Think about a picture you have hanging in your home. Now, imagine that same picture in a different frame. The picture looks different because the new frame changes your perspective. Now, think about a difficult experience from your past. With the passage of time, we often reframe that event by realizing it was really a good thing. For example, say you got fired from a job. As you reflect on the experience, you might say, "If I hadn't gotten fired from that job, I would never have gone back to school and learned that new skill and gotten this great new job." *Reframing* is the ability to find the gains that are hidden in the difficulty. By practicing reframing when you are in the midst of a trying situation, you identify the possible gains that might come from the event. You can then focus on these positives and balance out the crisis and the negative feelings. You basically say: "Yes, this is hard. Yes, this is frustrating, but I am going to get something out of the experience that will help me in the future." What I'm suggesting is that when you're having difficulty in the present, concentrate on the gains rather than the current problem. Think about what is happening in the present day as if you were looking back at it and appreciating how you benefited from the experience. By reframing the event, you're finding a perspective that motivates you to move on when bad things occur. Reframing works best with day-to-day stressors and frustrations. I'll talk about overcoming devastating events, such as death, in the next section.

Remember Nick, my old fiancé? When I returned to the U.S. after breaking off our engagement, I was devastated. I had lost my relationship and was feeling really bad about my body and myself on top of it. It was very painful and took a while to get over. Now, looking back, I can see that I learned a lot about what I needed in relationships from that experience. I was forced to work through my negative feelings about my body and realize that I had to make myself happy rather than expecting a relationship to do it for me. Also, when I came back, I began to work in addiction counseling and established a career in that area. All of these things might have happened eventually, but the negative experience with Nick *forced* them to happen. The benefits were not obvious at the time of Nick's and my breakup but became clear in hindsight.

I use this experience with Nick as a reminder that difficult situations are really a catalyst for my examining my life and an opportunity to make choices and decisions that will enhance my future. POWER Optimists look for benefits and reframe difficulties into opportunities. They move ahead by viewing obstacles from a new angle and gaining new perspectives. They look for future advantages and look for personal payoffs.

Summing Up the Strategy

One of the key strategies for *Adopting a Positive Outlook* is to *give yourself credit for creating successes and experience setbacks as temporary and fixable*. In this way, you start creating an explanatory style that will place you on an upward spiral. The next time a situation is a success, take out a piece of paper and write the words: permanent, pervasive and personal. Use each word to explain your success. For example, you might write, "My success is permanent because I can succeed the next time, too." Stop and let this explanation take root. In the same manner, create a positive explanatory style in the face of setbacks. For example, if you go out on a date and it doesn't work out, explain this occurrence as temporary, specific and not entirely personal. In this way, you are bolstering your skills and talents as well as providing a buffer against life's stresses and disappointments.

The POWER Optimist *fully appreciates and looks for positive creations and occurrences of all dimensions.* There are so many wonderful things happening around us—both large and small—and it's important to recognize and value them. Saying thank you, appreciating nature and keeping a gratitude journal are all simple, yet effective, ways to increase appreciation for the world around us. Too often, we get caught up in the hassles and challenges of our everyday lives and either take good things for granted or fail to notice positive events in the ordinary and everyday. Building the capacity for gratitude and appreciation helps lift your mood and creates an upward spiral of energy and awareness. The next time you feel down or just "blah," try an experiment. Challenge yourself to find five things you appreciate, no matter how small. Write them down or stop to meditate on them. When you shift your focus, you shift your energy and mood.

Finally, *Adopting a Positive Outlook* involves *identifying potential gains and future advantages that result from current difficulties.* Striving to see the potential benefits and opportunities for growth in your day-to-day challenges helps keep things in perspective and helps you to find the motivating interpretation in a given event. On the other hand, if you look at worrisome situations as detrimental, harmful or useless, you create a view of your experiences that is bound to place you on a downward spiral. The next time you are faced with a situation that appears difficult, disappointing or frightening, pay attention to your reaction. Remember that your initial response of fear, frustration or anger is normal. The key is not to get stuck in these reactions. Find the potential for personal growth and gain. This might take time, or you might need some input from others, but you will feel a new charge of energy and hopefulness as a result.

GROWING YOUR RESILIENT PRACTICE	
Adopting a Positive Outlook	
GROWTH SLUMP	GROWTH SURGE
Discount your role in successes yet view setbacks as personal failures.	Give yourself credit for creating successes and experience setbacks as temporary and fixable.
Take for granted or fail to notice ordinary and commonplace positive events.	Fully appreciate and look for positive creations and occurrences of all dimensions.
Look at worrisome situations as detrimental, harmful or useless.	Identify potential gains and future advantages that result from current difficulties.

REGULATING EMOTIONS

I will never forget a comment my own therapist said to me when I was in therapy in my early thirties. Overwhelmed by my own emotional life, I found her comment hard to believe. Now, I pass it along to my clients: "Your feelings are your friends." How can this be? Basically, an emotion is a *carrier of meaning*. When you feel one of the four basic emotions—joy, anger, sadness, fear—the emotion is communicating something to you.

The first step in figuring out what the emotion is trying to tell you is to ask yourself, "What am I feeling?" This may sound strange, but it can be hard to identify exactly what you're feeling when strong emotions are involved. For example, fear can seem a lot like anger when you're overwhelmed. Anger may, in fact, be masking sadness. Once you have identified the feeling, the next step is to uncover the meaning. If you are experiencing joy, you know you are getting what you need, want and desire. Ask yourself, "How did I help create this situation and how can I continue to maintain this circumstance?" If, however, you are feeling flooded by anger, it is likely that you are being blocked from getting what you need or want. Ask yourself, "What can I do to get what I need?" If you are feeling sadness, it is likely that you have lost something that you needed or wanted. Ask yourself, "How can I replace it?" If you are feeling fear, it is likely that you feel threatened with the loss of something or someone you need or want. Ask yourself, "What can I do if I lose this?"

What is the emotion trying to tell you? Once you have the answer to that question, you can start to make a plan or move ahead. When experiencing fear, anger or sadness, your task is to feel the feeling, understand it and then let it go by finding a remedy for the situation. To prevent yourself from getting trapped in a downward spiral, it's critical to release the negative energy so that you can replace it with something more positive. Only you can do this. No one else can release negative energy for you. Only you can find the meaning and release the feeling so that it doesn't bother you anymore.

The key to finding the meaning in your emotions is self-awareness and self-observation. Pay attention to your physical sensations when you are experiencing joy, fear, sadness or anger. Learn how your body feels in these emotional states. Observe your thoughts and behaviors and learn how your feelings affect your thoughts and actions. By being a neutral observer and practicing self-awareness, you develop emotional literacy: the ability to know what you are feeling and why. When you are emotionally literate, you understand what's important to you, how you experience positive and negative events, how you react under stress, what situations "push your buttons" and how you react to other people.

When fate hands us a lemon, let's try to make lemonade.
—Dale Carnegie

By increasing your emotional literacy, you become well-informed and well-versed in your own emotional life, which gives you the ability to regulate your emotions. It doesn't matter whether you think about regulating your emotional life by *going for the upward spiral* or by *avoiding the downward spiral*. Both approaches put you in charge of your emotions in order to create conditions for success and well-being. In the process of learning how to regulate your emotions, you will discover that there are some techniques that are particularly effective for you, while others are less useful. Take what is useful to you and apply it to your life so you can maintain a forward momentum. Here are some effective ways to regulate your emotions.

Be prepared for backlash. How many times do you find yourself on an upward spiral, only to wonder why you can't stay there? Here's one reason why: old patterns are comfortable, as you remember from the discussion about eradicating schemas. People often experience a backlash when they try to change negative patterns and regulate their emotions. This happens because negative patterns and emotions want to stay active and powerful in our lives. It can feel uncomfortable to act or react differently than you are used to doing. You need to be prepared for your negative patterns and emotions to reappear so that you can deal with them effectively if they do. Assess whether the negative emotions are the result of emotional hijacks, schemas or other unhealthy patterns of response. Recognizing the negative pattern will remind you that you are in control, and you don't have to react in a negative way. You can shape your reactions to the event in the way you want.

Release negative emotions. The fact is, emotions and upsets can linger without actually being valid. Research shows that negative emotions often persist beyond their usefulness. The bodily conditions that accompany negative emotions, such as irritability and increases in heart rate and blood pressure, continue even after we have uncovered the meaning behind the emotion. Allowing negative emotions to control your thoughts and actions is one sure way to leave an upward spiral or to remain on a downward spiral. When a negative emotion becomes prolonged, use one of the strategies below to let it go.

- *Feel the feelings.* You can experience your feelings without trying to affect them. Don't judge the feelings, try to change them or fix them. Allow whatever is happening just to be, like the clouds passing in the sky. Ride out the emotions, and they will pass. Try exploring the feeling with openness and curiosity. Ask yourself, "What is happening? What does it feel like?" As you intentionally observe the sensation, it will begin to change. By feeling your feelings, the energy of the feeling is released and you learn that you don't have to react.[4]

- *Divert your mental attention.* As a way of shifting your emotions, shift the focus of your attention. Pay attention to what is happening around you in the present moment. One way to do this is a strategy called "3-2-1, see-hear-feel," which helps divert attention away from overwhelming or negative feelings. In this strategy, use your attention to identify three things you can see; three things that you can hear; and three things that you can physically feel. For example, you might look around you and see a sparrow, a red car and a small child. You might listen intently and hear the cars outside, the radio playing downstairs and the cat meowing, and you might feel the chair you're sitting on, the breeze on your face, and the coffee cup in your hand. Then, identify two things you see-hear-feel, and then one of each. Use this when you are getting hijacked as a way to orient you to the present moment and distract you from overwhelming emotion.

- *Take action.* Interrupt the feeling with action. The action you take can be connected to the situation that is upsetting you. For example, you might decide that you are going to write a letter to the person who hurt you, even if you never end up sending it. Your action can be something completely unrelated, like cleaning your bathroom, exercising, filing some paperwork or baking a cake. You might want to soothe yourself by engaging in a relaxing activity such as taking a long, hot bath or going for a walk. The important thing is to get up and do something, shake up your mind and emotions and work through the feeling.

- *Tap into the positive.* Apply a positive interpretation to the negative emotions. Think of how you might look back on this particular upset in a year's time and reframe the current event in a way that highlights the benefits that can occur. You might cultivate positive emotions like joy and amusement by remembering a time that brings a smile to your face. You can also produce the tranquil positive emotions of serenity and appreciation by getting out your gratitude log or visualizing a beautiful sunset. The ability to cultivate positive emotions is a powerful skill for regulating negative emotions.

Beware of faulty connections. We make faulty connections when we have an emotion and attach a patterned negative thought to that emotion. Everyday life is full of stressful events that produce feelings such as sadness, anxiety, loneliness or anger. We often are unaware of these feelings and don't have time to process them, so they can build up and overwhelm us. Because we are already feeling negative, the tendency is to attach a negative thought to the feelings. The easiest place to find a connection is with our pre-existing negative patterns. Usually, the feeling gets attached to our limiting beliefs or schemas because these are our default mechanisms for explaining the world. In my case, for example, when I feel bad, my default mechanism says it must be because I'm not good enough or I'm too fat, so that becomes my explanation for what's going on, which only reinforces my negative pattern. Avoid placing yourself on a downward spiral by attaching negative patterned thoughts to your emotions.

Don't ruminate. Rumination happens when you keep thinking and feeling the same, old, negative thoughts, even though they aren't helping you. It's a form of emotional obsession and, like all obsessions, traps and controls the individual. Don't keep unhealthy and unproductive feelings alive by dwelling on the negative. Instead, if you feel the urge to ruminate, try thought-stopping. Notice the thought, and then dismiss it by saying to yourself "Stop!" Replace the thought in your mind with a positive thought or affirmation. If you feel yourself obsessing, move on to problem solving. Ask yourself what concrete steps you can take to remedy the situation and focus on these actions. Another tactic is to visualize your negative thoughts in a helium balloon and then release the balloon—and your thoughts—into the air. Finally, rather than ruminate, activate. Go out and do something active to distract yourself.

Summing Up the Strategy

To *Regulate Emotions* means *developing emotional literacy so you can take charge of your emotions.* This requires self-awareness and self-observation. Practice paying attention to what you feel and why. Become aware of what kinds of situations push your buttons. Observe your responses to learn new ways to regulate your reactions. If you don't learn these things about yourself, you will essentially be allowing your emotions to rule your life. Rather than be at the mercy of your emotions, discover what to expect from yourself when unplanned or unpleasant things happen. By developing emotional literacy, you can learn to read your emotions so they can help you be resilient in the face of the unexpected.

One of the key strategies to *Regulating Emotions* is *be prepared when negative patterns and emotions show up and release them.* Remember, you may experience a backlash of your negative patterns as you move forward. Take charge by reminding yourself that this is part of the process so these patterned emotions don't control your life. When you experience negative emotions and have ascertained their meaning, it's time to move on. Don't let the impact of negative emotions linger and take over. Instead, go for the upward spiral by releasing the negative.

Finally, *Regulating Emotions* means *going for an upward spiral by maintaining positive emotions.* This involves diverting your attention from the negative or soothing yourself with positive actions. Going for the upward spiral also means interrupting any tendencies to dwell on negative thoughts, as rumination only re-energizes negative feelings and patterns. Be vigilant for faulty connections of negative thoughts and negative feelings, as this only distracts you from finding the motivating interpretation behind the emotions, placing you on a downward spiral. Instead, actively cultivate energized positive emotions, such as joy and amusement or tranquil positive emotions, such as serenity and appreciation. By actively regulating your emotions, you maintain an upward spiral of energy and resiliency.

GROWING YOUR RESILIENT PRACTICE	
Regulating Emotions	
GROWTH SLUMP	**GROWTH SURGE**
Permit your emotions to rule your life.	Develop emotional literacy so you can take charge of your emotions.
Allow old negative patterns and emotions to take over.	Be prepared when negative patterns and emotions show up and release them.
Produce a downward spiral by "faulty connections" and "rumination."	Go for an upward spiral by maintaining positive emotions and releasing negative emotions.

FINDING MEANING IN ADVERSITY

In the course of our lives, we will all experience pain and suffering. This section addresses life events that are more debilitating than the day-to-day challenges discussed in the previous section. These include life experiences that are extraordinarily stressful and difficult, such as divorce, death, fire, accidents and financial crisis. Some experiences cause suffering so severe as to be traumatic. Examples might include being physically or emotionally victimized, having to flee one's home or country because of war or civil unrest, losing a child or loved one to assault or a traumatic accident or experiencing a severe health problem.

Adversity and trauma, while terrible, can also be a stepping-stone to positive growth and maturity *when one is able to find meaning in the adversity*. You may not need to apply the lessons in this section at this time, and it is my hope that you will be spared the kind of pain that accompanies severely traumatic experiences. The information provided here can be used as a resource in times of need and an example of how others have coped with experiences that might, on their face, appear to be insurmountable.

Many people who have experienced adversity discover that these life events, strangely enough, helped them to develop a sense of perspective and scale, taught them empathy and tolerance for others and enabled them to behave more lovingly than they believed possible. Surviving adversity and trauma informs people of their true nature and the essence of their humanity. Those who have experienced traumatic events speak about their profound realizations of the importance of kindness, the power of love and their appreciation for what remains. It appears that this level of insight often comes from suffering.

Holocaust survivor Victor Frankl wrote extensively on the role of suffering in the creation of meaning. Best known for his work, *Man's Search for Meaning*, Frankl believed that *meaning* consists of knowledge and personal insight into what it means to really be oneself. Frankl was a successful Austrian psychiatrist who lost everything precious to him in World War II. Aside from one sister, everyone in Frankl's immediate family perished in the Nazi death camps. He lost his parents, brother and wife. He lost his home and his possessions. While imprisoned, Frankl developed his theory, called logotherapy, which states that the most important thing a person has is the sense that his or her life has meaning and value. The loss of this sense of meaning is unbearable for most people. In the concentration camps, Frankl noted that many gave up hope when their lives were deprived of meaning.

Frankl believed that every life has meaning, even under the most terrible conditions, and that every person has an innate desire to find meaning in life. In fact, a person's most important task in life is to discover the meaning of his or her own life. What's more, he believed we all have the freedom to do so regardless of our circumstances. Frankl suggested that we can find meaning in any of three ways that are connected to our creations, our experiences or our suffering.[5]

- *Creative Values*: Meaning can be found through what we contribute to the world by our actions, our creations and our efforts in the world. This is the case when we work, volunteer, create or act in the world.

- *Experiential Values*: Meaning may be found in how we experience life and what we take from it. This includes appreciating art, reveling in nature and loving people for their unique qualities.

- *The Third Doorway*: Meaning may be found even in the most terrible situation by our response to—and attitude about—the situation itself. This is the case for those denied the opportunity to find creative or experiential value in their lives due to illness, incarceration or other barriers. The Third Doorway allows individuals to choose their response to their situation, regardless of how much control they have over the situation itself.

> *Everything can be taken from a man but…the last of the human freedoms, to choose one's attitude in any given set of circumstances, to choose one's own way.* —Victor Frankl

While being imprisoned in a concentration camp is an extreme and horrible experience, there are many lessons for us in Frankl's work. Adversity can lead to positive growth and the discovery of abilities and strengths you never knew you had. While you wouldn't seek out such negative experiences, when the adversity or trauma is unavoidable, Frankl's philosophy can help you deal with pain and find a meaning that brings value and a sense of purpose to your experience.

A recent study interviewed parents who had lost a child and explored how the parents had fared after the experience. It turned out that many had created meaning from this experience, despite the fact that it was terrible to lose a child. Those who were coping the best had created a positive interpretation of the event, one that focused on growth rather than despair. They had been able to take the experience of loss and integrate it into their experience in a positive way. These parents reported that they felt more appreciative of life in general and more grateful for their life specifically. They were more compassionate, more aware of the importance of other loved ones in their lives and more interested in helping others or society. Compared to parents who were not faring as well, the highly functioning parents had a greater understanding of life and death and lived each day to the fullest. They had stronger faith and were more aware of the preciousness of life. They had come through the trauma of their child's death and had managed to find meaning from the experience that changed their own lives for the better.[6]

Suffering with meaning = positive growth and maturity
Suffering without meaning = no growth, despair

It is essential to remember that traumatic or unexpected and life-altering events very often require a period of grieving and readjustment before using POWER Optimism or other cognitive behavior therapy strategies. Americans are, in general, uncomfortable with grief and mourning. In a country where most employees get, at most, three days of bereavement leave if a family member passes away, it can be hard to fully honor the grieving process and move through all of the phases of grief.

The process of recovering from bereavement has three stages. First, there is an initial phase of shock or numbness. This phase is characterized by protests about what has happened, denial of the importance of the events and longing for the past. The second phase is disorganization and disorientation. During this period, the individual feels alone, uncertain and confused. The final stage is known as recovery, or reorganization. At this point, the individual begins to integrate what has happened into his or her life, accommodate the events into his or her worldview and discover new relationships and outlets. Everyone grieves in his or her own way. When a person experiences a traumatic event or loss, it is critical to acknowledge what has been lost and to go through these stages in the way that makes sense for the individual. Too often, however, people try to rush the stages and pretend or force themselves to act as if everything is all right when it really isn't.

Another common problem that interferes with healing is the expectation that one's life and personality will eventually regain the same characteristics they had before. Traumatic and severe losses are usually life-changing. This is because the process involves restructuring the way you think about the world as well as readjusting and revising your life to accommodate the new events or situation. It is critical to note that you are unlikely to be the same as you were before the traumatic event or loss. Expecting everything to be the same, even after time has passed, is not realistic and holding on to such an expectation may prevent you from recovering fully. The reality is that dealing with adversity and trauma changes the way you experience yourself and your role in the world.

Pulling through trauma and loss can be accelerated by searching for the meaning of the experience. While grieving is a highly individual process, the time may be right to start finding a motivating interpretation of the experience as you move through the disorientation stage and into the recovery stage. In this way, you can begin to develop a sense of purpose that can help you transform suffering into meaning and allow you to concentrate on the future again. Here are some questions to ask yourself when you have experienced adversity in your life. Answering these questions will help you work through the event, make sense of its role in your life and find a motivating interpretation to promote your healing from the event.

1. Who am I now in the face of this adversity?

2. How am I different?

3. What is important about me?

4. Do I see life in a new way?

5. Do I envision my future in a different way?

6. Do I have a new purpose for being?

7. How can I construct the meaning and purpose of my life?

8. What is my new role in life?

> The difference between stumbling blocks and stepping-stones is in how you use them.   —*Welsh proverb*

Summing Up the Strategy

One of the key concepts for *Finding Meaning in Adversity* is to *recognize the innate desire to find meaning in suffering.* If you focus solely on your pain, you hinder your healing by zeroing in on the negative. You block your ability to uncover the meaning of the suffering. Concentrating on suffering to the exclusion of everything else in life is not compatible with growth and recovery. Remember, you have an inborn desire and the personal freedom to uncover your own meaning. Open yourself up to finding meaning through creative means, by experiential activities or from your own personal responses to the situation. While this takes time and effort, the benefits are profound and include a renewed sense of and appreciation for life.

Finding Meaning in Adversity rests on the foundation of *honoring your individual process of grieving.* Just as focusing solely on pain and grief hinders your healing, so too does denying your pain. Too often people try to negate their pain and move beyond it without really experiencing their grief or fully healing from their loss. If you bury your head in the sand and avoid dealing with the pain, you block your healing by short-circuiting the grieving process. Remember, grieving is an individual process. There is no right way to move through the stages, and not everyone experiences the stages in the same way. The key is to experience your grief while you simultaneously stay open to your own resiliency.

Finally, *Finding Meaning in Adversity* involves *practicing self-reflection to uncover and identify opportunities for growth and change.* Growth does not come without exertion. It takes a concentrated effort to think about the meaning of your life, especially if you are experiencing a traumatic and stressful event, but it is at precisely these moments that you are able to see beyond yourself and to understand the profundity of life. The desire to search for meaning is potent, but it can be overridden by feelings of powerlessness or hopelessness. It is important not to give into these stifling and restricting impulses and to push through the pain to discover a motivating interpretation. Take the time to reflect on questions that speak to the core of your being, the values you hold dear and the fundamental aspects of your life purpose. These kinds of questions will help unlock the meaning of your suffering and promote personal growth and positive change.

GROWING YOUR RESILIENT PRACTICE	
Finding Meaning in Adversity	
GROWTH SLUMP	**GROWTH SURGE**
Focus solely on the suffering of adversity and trauma.	Recognize the innate desire to find meaning in suffering.
Ignore or shorten your grieving process.	Honor your individual process of grieving.
Allow powerlessness or hopelessness to divert your search for meaning.	Practice self-reflection to uncover and identify opportunities for growth and change.

In the aftermath of natural disasters, such as floods, gardens exhibit their resiliency. With care taken to clean up debris and repair damaged plants, optimum growth can be expected. When facing the hardships of life, people need care, too. We need to clean up the leftover hurt and frustration, repair the damage to our hearts and souls. We need to nurture our resiliency with positivity, appreciation and meaning— allowing our optimum potential to unfold even in difficult and trying times. Like the plants in the garden, with nurturance, we can move forward and reclaim life as we work through challenges.

3

Maintaining Your Garden

Chapter Nine

How Does Your Garden Grow?
Reaping Optimum Rewards

Gardens can transform dirt into beauty. Unused, blighted spaces are converted into lush jewels. Optimism has the potential to take the barren spaces of our lives and convert them into a terrain filled with success, pleasure and joy. All that is required from us to reap these benefits is to shift our focus to the positive, to put our attention on what we want to create and to stay on the path that is right for us.

After listening to a presentation on POWER Optimism, an audience member remarked, "You make it sound so easy, but doesn't it take a lot of work?" My answer was one word. "Yes!" Cultivating optimism can result in a life that is filled with rewards, but it does take effort. You have to ready the soil for planting POWER Optimism by pulling the weeds of limiting beliefs, past events, schemas and emotional hijacks, and then you need to plant the seeds of your optimism by using strategies to become Proactive, Open-minded, Well-informed, Evolving and Resilient.

Of course, you want to reap the optimum rewards for your efforts. Up to this point, you've learned specific tools to release your negative patterns and create positive practices. Now it's time to get ideas on how to use these tools to their best advantage. The ideas and activities in this chapter will keep you motivated and energized as you hone your POWER Optimism skills. They are designed to help you maximize opportunities to thrive and flourish, so you can enjoy the life you have and create the life you want.

KEEP PULLING THE WEEDS

Changing our lives and the way we respond to people and things around us is a complicated and time-consuming process. It's unrealistic to expect that anyone can immediately and instantly alter personal habits, many of which, as we've seen, have been ingrained since youth. Negative habits are pathways in our brains and are rooted in our beings. As a result, they have an enormous amount of pull. Weeds can creep into our gardens not just from our past. We live in a culture that is choked with weeds. Families, schools, the media and entertainment industry all have positive aspects, but they can also reinforce negativity or plant poor habits in our lives. Consumerism, intolerance, bigotry and greed are just a few of the cultural factors that also produce and reinforce negative patterns. Our negative patterns keep creeping back into our lives, just like the weeds that keep creeping back into a garden.

If you want to really eliminate your negative patterns, you must be prepared to continue using the weeding tools described in Chapter Three. This can at first be discouraging. After all, you've just worked so hard on letting go of your negative patterns, and here they are—back again! Maintain a realistic expectation that the weeds will return. Remember the three watchwords for changing a habit: frequency, intensity and duration. Look for changes in your patterns. Remember that the old patterns continue to exist in conjunction with the new patterns you are trying to instill. Over time, you will notice that the new habit is becoming stronger in relation to the old habit. At first, maybe you notice the old habit exists 90% of the time, then 70%, then it's 50-50. With more practice, the new habit is now present 70% of the time, then 80%, then 95%. What a difference!

Here are some activities that can help you keep the weeds out of your garden—whether they come from within or without.

> *We are what we repeatedly do.*
> *Excellence, then is not an act but a habit.*
> —Aristotle

Relaxation Breathing

The purpose of this activity is to quiet your thoughts and anxieties so that you can concentrate on changing your negative patterns. As you calm your breathing, your thoughts will also become more measured, enabling you to let go of negative feelings and become less agitated. Relaxation can help you gain perspective on your life and help recharge your battery as you work on forming new habits. Here's how it works:

- Breathe in through your nose for a count of four.
- Hold your breath for a count of seven (count slowly: one thousand one, one thousand two, etc.).
- Exhale for a count of eight (again, count slowly).

Nature: Letting Go

For this activity, you will need to find things from the natural world and work with them symbolically. Spend some time outdoors gathering articles that you can use to create an object which represents the negative thoughts, feelings or behaviors you want to release. For example, you might bring home some sticks to make a bundle. You might glue leaves to some paper or thread acorns together on a string. Regardless of what you create, think about the negativity you are currently facing as you create your item. Now, it is time to let go of this negativity. Destroy your creation and, as you do so, let go of your negative thoughts, feelings and behaviors. You might bury it, burn it or throw it in a river. However you let go of the item, think very consciously about letting go of your negativity at the same time.

Drawing

Drawing is a good strategy because it engages the entire brain, using both right and left hemispheres. For this activity, draw a room. Inside the room, draw things that give you strength and comfort and that put you in a positive and energetic frame of mind. These are things or people that counter your negativity and negative patterns. Outside the room, draw the negative things and people that bring you down and threaten your growth of POWER Optimism. It's OK if the drawing looks silly or not very skilled. The point here is not to produce a great work of art but to make your brain flow and release ideas that will motivate and encourage you to shift your focus from the negative to the positive.

Be Your Own Expert

Imagine you are your own mentor and give yourself advice. Often, we know exactly what we need to do to create an upward spiral, but we get caught up in our own blind spots and destructive patterns. Many times, my clients tell me that when they don't know what to do they ask themselves "What would Dana say?" They then imagine my advice and proceed from there. The advice is actually coming from them, because they have internalized the information and changes we have been working on. This exercise is about imagining you are the therapist or friend giving advice. What POWER Optimism tools would you suggest to release the negative pattern? What could you suggest that would shift energy from the downward spiral to an upward one?

Opportunities to find deeper powers within ourselves come when life seems most challenging.
—Joseph Campbell

FERTILIZE THE SOIL AND WATER THE PLANTS

If you want your garden to grow beautifully, you not only need to keep the ground clear and prevent toxins from destroying the plants, you also need to provide nutrients and care to the garden. If you want your optimism to really blossom, it's essential to nurture the seeds you plant. It's not enough to just know about the strategies. You need to practice them regularly. In fact, even when there are no obvious problems confronting you, keep working on the strategies. In this way, you will become proficient at them, and you will reap greater benefits. Eventually, the strategies will become automatic. They will be rooted in your life.

As you practice the strategies of POWER Optimism, they will become unique to you. Because everyone is different, you will discover new aspects of the five Practices for yourself. It's like training for a sport: each athlete learns techniques and then implements the knowledge individually to suit his or her needs and talents. Use the Practices regularly, and they will be shaped in the way that will most assist you to create opportunities for success and well-being.

At first, it can seem overwhelming to implement all of the strategies. To keep yourself on track, pick three of the various strategies described in the Practices. Photocopy the *Growth Spurt-Growth Slump* charts from these three strategies and read them every day to remind yourself of what they say. Keep a daily or weekly journal of how you have used the strategies and any changes you see in your life or your interpretation of events around you. Do this for a month with the three target strategies and then pick three more strategies. You could also stick with the same three strategies or just change or add one or two new strategies to work on in the coming month.

Here are other suggestions that will help you nourish your skills and promote self-growth.

Anchor the Strategy

"Anchoring the strategy" involves creating a habit to help you reinforce a chosen strategy. An "anchor" is an activity you can do easily and repeatedly, such as squeezing your thumb and index finger together or touching your wrist. First, decide what activity you'll use as an anchor. Then, pick a POWER Optimism strategy that you want to practice. It can be one that you've successfully used in the past or one that you can imagine using successfully in the future. Actively think about the success of this strategy, either by remembering how it worked for you in the past or *imagining* how it could be helpful. Then, pay active attention to all of your senses and your emotions as you recall or imagine the experience of successfully working the strategy. As you experience the positive, upward energy that accompanies success, set the anchor by doing the activity you had selected before. If it was to squeeze your thumb and index finger together, do that as you are actively remembering the feeling of success. Now, test the anchor. Repeat the action (e.g. squeeze your thumb and index finger together), and see if positive energy surfaces. If it doesn't, it just means you set the anchor too soon or too late. Go back, re-experience the positive energy, and set the anchor again. Once the anchor is set, whenever you need to recall the strategy and the accompanying feelings of success, all you need to do is repeat the action that set the anchor, and you will get a feeling of positive emotion and success.

Cheerleaders

This is a visualization activity. Think about people in your life who are appreciative and supportive of you. These people are your cheerleaders who give you kudos and help you strive to achieve your goals. Visualize these cheerleaders standing around you and imagine that you are telling them about an accomplishment or a time you were successful in your life. After you've imagined your accomplishment, imagine your cheerleaders applauding you and patting you on the back. Absorb the positive energy from this activity and use it to motivate you to try new POWER Optimism strategies. Whatever you would like to try—but feel nervous about attempting—imagine that you have already done it and are telling the cheerleaders about the experience. Their support will help you make the extra effort to get up and go.

Make a Collage

Drawing and the visual arts are a great way to tap into energy and ideas. Making a collage about your life and/or feelings is a fun way to express yourself as well. For this activity, choose a comfortable place and select a period when you have some free time. You will need magazines and catalogs, scissors, paste and large paper or poster board. Go through the magazines and cut out pictures and words that appeal to you. These might be pictures that represent things in your life, like your pet or your dream vacation home. They might be illustrations that tap into ideas of activities you'd like to try, or the pictures and words might represent excitement, success or fun. They might be pretty or just appealing to you for no obvious reason. If an image or word appeals to you, tear it out and put it in a pile. Once you think you have enough material, arrange them on the paper. The final image doesn't have to be museum-quality. It just needs to be about you and contain pictures or words that you like. Collages can celebrate successes, show goals or just act as a snapshot of a certain moment in time. Put your collage up somewhere where you can see it regularly and reflect on it.

WELCOME THE RAIN AND ENJOY THE SUNSHINE

What happens when you change your attitude? What is the end result when you incorporate the tools and strategies of the POWER Optimism program? The answer: *Nothing has changed, but everything is altered.* Your life will still be filled with its disappointments, frustrations, anxieties and worries. Setbacks and frustrations are a normal part of life. If everything always went smoothly, there would be no need for POWER Optimism. In fact, without the contrast of difficult times, it is hard to appreciate the good times and accomplishments of our lives, so becoming a POWER Optimist will not prevent the rain. There will still be setbacks and obstacles you will have to face, but as a POWER Optimist, you will now welcome the rain because you know that you can learn and grow when challenged and work to overcome obstacles. You know you don't have to get stuck in the negative. You now have the power to create interpretations and responses that will help you gain the most from the experience and move on in your life. Nothing has changed. You will still have problems, but everything is altered because you can now take a difficulty and use it to your own advantage.

> *You may be disappointed if you fail,*
> *but you are doomed if you don't try.*
> —*Beverly Sills*

When you become a POWER Optimist, you not only handle difficulties differently, you also approach the positive from a different perspective. POWER Optimism gives you the tools you need to experience the good things in life more fully. When something good happens, you now enjoy the experience full tilt. No more brushing off your accomplishments with "yes, but." No more holding back your energy and enthusiasm. Instead, you intentionally seek out that upward spiral of success and well-being. You have developed the ability to fully notice, appreciate and live in every moment. Think about POWER Optimism as eating your favorite food. The food is still the same, but suddenly the taste is more intense.

As you become more optimistic, you will begin to notice that there are more positive opportunities available to you. How did this happen? In reality, nothing has changed. What has altered is that you now notice the opportunities that are available. Once you adopt a perspective of optimism, you more readily see the abundance that exists. This is because you have taken off the blinders of negativity that limit your horizons and vision. Instead of walking down the same path, you can choose the path that best suits your journey because you are looking for the path. The following account illustrates how we learn to create positive outcomes.

Autobiography in Five Short Chapters
By Portia Nelson

> *I.*

I walk down the street.

> *There is a deep hole in the sidewalk.*
> *I fall in.*
> *I am lost...............I am helpless.*
>> *It isn't my fault.*

I take forever to find a way out.

> *II.*

I walk down the street.

> *There is a deep hole in the sidewalk.*
> *I pretend I don't see it.*
> *I fall in, again.*

I can't believe I am in this same place.

>> *But, it isn't my fault.*

It takes a long time to get out.

> *III.*

I walk down the same street.

> *There is a deep hole in the sidewalk.*
> *I see it is there.*
> *I still fall in.......it's a habit........but,*
>> *My eyes are open.*
>> *I know where I am.*

It is my fault.
I get out immediately.

> *IV.*

I walk down the same street.

> *There is a deep hole in the sidewalk.*
> *I walk around it.*

> *V.*

I walk down another street.

I celebrate your decision to learn POWER Optimism and to embrace this exciting way of looking at the world. I hope you find the ideas, tools, strategies and activities in this book useful in creating the life you want. Enjoy the journey.

Chapter Ten

Gardening Tools—Additional Resources to Keep You Going

*Gardeners work hard and having the right tools can help.
As we cultivate POWER Optimism, tapping into additional resources
can make our progress easier and more inspiring.*

In the course of learning and practicing POWER Optimism, you may want to explore in greater depth some of the ideas presented in this book. There is an abundance of first rate material available, and the books listed here make excellent reading. I have provided a brief description of each book to help your selection process. If a book is particularly relevant to a tool or strategy of the POWER Optimism program, I have indicated that information so you can find resources on specific topics you want to investigate. Use these publications as supplemental tools to cultivate the growth and development of your optimism.

Bennett-Goleman, T. (2001). *Emotional Alchemy: How the Mind Can Heal the Heart.* NY: Harmony Books. → *Schemas* Uses the practice of mindfulness and meditation to teach how to free yourself from ten basic emotional patterns.

Branden, N. (1994). *The Six Pillars of Self-Esteem.* NY: Bantam. → *Self-Acceptance* Six action-based practices with exercises to increase personal awareness and effectiveness.

Childe, D. and Martin, H. (1999). *The Heartmath Solution.* San Francisco: Harper. → *Releasing Emotional Hijacks* Provides research on the impact of the heart on emotions, mind and physical health with techniques to channel the heart's intelligence.

Covey, S. R. (1990). *The 7 Habits of Highly Effective People* NY: Fireside Books. → *Proactive* Presents a holistic, integrated, principle-centered approach for solving personal and professional problems.

Elliott, C. H. and Lassen, M. K. (1998). *Why Can't I Get What I Want? How to Stop Making the Same Old Mistakes and Start Living a Life You Can Love.* Palo Alto: Davies Black Publishing. → *Schemas* Shows how to identify maladaptive schemas and develop adaptive strategies to replace them.

Ford, Debbie. (1998). *The Dark Side of the Light Chasers.* NY: Riverhead Books. → *Past Events* Describes how to acknowledge and accept our so-called weaknesses and turn them into important, hidden strengths.

Frankl, V. E. (1963). *Man's Search for Meaning.* NY: Simon and Schuster. → *Resiliency* Tells the story of Frankl's imprisonment at Auschwitz and his resultant development of logotherapy, describing how to find the purpose in one's life.

Gershon, D. & Staub, G. (1989). *Empowerment: The Art of Creating Your Life As You Want It.* NY: High Point Press. →

Limiting Beliefs An easy-to-use guide describing tools to achieve what you desire out of life.

Grabhorn, Lynn. (2000). *Excuse Me. Your Life is Waiting.* Charlottesville, VA: Hampton Roads Publishing Co., Inc. → *Changing feelings* Discusses how to produce feelings to attract what you want to create in your life.

Goleman, Daniel. (1995). *Emotional Intelligence.* NY: Bantam Books. → *Emotional Hijacks* Describes a different way of being smart based on emotional skills and how to nurture and strengthen these skills.

Hendricks, Gay. (2002). *Achieving Vibrance.* NY: Three Rivers Press. → *Changing feelings* Teaches a program to restore and optimize the harmonious feelings of your "original" youth.

Kane, A. & Kane, S. (1999). *Working on Yourself Doesn't Work.* NY: ASK Publications. → *Releasing Negative Patterns* Teaches how to transform your life by getting into and living from the moment—this current moment of "now."

Kabat-Zinn, J. (1991). *Full Catastrophe Living.* NY: Dell Publishing Co. → *Neutral Observer* A practical guide to mindfulness and meditation, explaining how to develop moment-to-moment awareness.

Luskin, Fred. (2002). *Forgive for Good.* San Francisco: Harper. → *Past Events* Offers a nine-step forgiveness method to move beyond being a victim to a life of contentment and peace.

McGinnis, A. L. (1987). *The Power of Optimism.* San Francisco: Harper & Row. → *Gives* twelve basic traits that distinguish optimists and steps for incorporating them into your life.

McGraw, P.C. (1999). *Life Strategies: Doing What Works, Doing What Matters.* NY: Hyperion. → *Maintaining Personal Accountability* Lists the Ten Laws of Life with strategies and assignments to put them into practice.

Mercer, M. & Troiani, M. (1998). *Spontaneous Optimism.* Lake Zurich, Illinois: Castlegate Publishers, Inc. → *Releasing Negative Patterns* Teaches simple techniques to quickly develop an optimistic attitude and lifestyle, especially in the areas of health, prosperity and happiness.

Norem, J. K. (2001). *The Positive Power of Negative Thinking.* Cambridge, MA: Basic Books. → Describes maladaptive features of optimism in contrast with defensive pessimism, which shares many features of the POWER Optimism™ practices.

Pierce, P. (1997). *The Intuitive Way.* Hillsboro, OR: Beyond Words Publishing. → Describes the intuitive process as a new way of life and demonstrates practical applications from speeding decision making to expanding personal growth.

Perry, J.M. (1997). *The Road to Optimism.* San Ramon, CA: Manfit Press. → *Role of Language* Describes the use of language and its impact on optimistic attitudes.

Rosanoff, N. (1991). *Intuition Workout.* Boulder Creek, CA: Aslan Publishing. → An 8-week program that teaches you to access your "deepest knowing" immediately, whenever you need it.

Seligman, M. (1990). *Learned Optimism.* NY: Pocketbooks. *Adopting a Positive Attitude* → Shows you how to recognize your "explanatory style" and provides techniques to transform negative thoughts.

Seligman, M. (2002). *Authentic Happiness.* NY: Free Press. → Describes the growing field of positive psychology and how to apply these concepts in your life.

Snyder, C.R. (1994). *The Psychology of Hope.* NY: The Free Press. *Setting and Achieving Goals* → Focuses on the ability to set and achieve goals as the distinguishing features of hopeful people and describes methods to become proficient in utilizing goals.

Tiger, L. (1979). *Optimism: The Biology of Hope.* NY: Kodansha

International. → Argues that optimism is not an optional characteristic but a biological phenomenon to support the survival of humans.

Young, J. E. & Klosko, J. S. (1993). *Reinventing Your Life.* NY: Plume. → *Schemas* Describes eleven schemas (or lifetraps) and how to break free of them.

Vaughan, S. C. (2000). *Half Empty, Half Full.* NY: Harcourt, Inc. → *Role of Emotions* Examines the origins of optimism in early life and the role of biology in how we interpret our experience and offers techniques to fool the brain into looking on the bright side.

Zander, R. S. & Zander, B. (2000). *The Art of Possibility.* Boston: HBS Press. → *Role of Interpretation* Gives 12 practices based on two premises—that life is composed as a story and that, with new definitions, much more is possible in our lives.

Notes

Chapter One

[1] You can read more about optimism research in Martin Seligman, *Learned Optimism*. Also, visit Dr. Seligman's website at *www.authentichappiness.org*.

[2] Martin Seligman, *Authentic Happiness* (Free Press, 2002), p. 24.

[3] I first read about the notion of unrealistic optimism in a description of dynamic optimism, which is a combination of philosophical understanding and psychological knowledge put forth by Max More, Ph.D. For more information see Max More, *Dynamic Optimism: An Extropian Cognitive-Emotional Virtue* (1998) or visit online at *www.maxmore.com*.

[4] If you are interested in resources for starting and running your own business, the Small Business Administration has a website at *www.sba.gov*.

Chapter Two

[1] See Mary Sykes and Richard Simon, "Discoveries from the Black Box," and Brent Atkinson, "Brain to Brain," which both appear in *Psychotherapy Networker*, (September/October, 2002). These articles are excellent overviews on recent brain research and present information on neural pathways and their role in our thought and reactive processes.

[2] For a discussion on the power of interpretation in determining our mood states, see M. Seligman, *Authentic Happiness* (Free Press, 2002).

[3] To learn more about correct and incorrect connections and the brain's neural pathways, see Laura Markowitz, "Wake Up Your Brain," in *Psychotherapy Networker* (January/February, 1999).

4 If you are interested in information and background on this kind of psychotherapy, two excellent resources are: J. Schwartz and S. Begley, *The Mind and The Brain* (Regan Books, 2002) and *www.cognitivetherapy.com*.

5 Positive psychology is the latest model to focus on people's assets. Other therapeutic models that also work from an asset-based perspective include humanist, solution-focused, resilience-oriented and cognitive-behavioral psychology. For a good review see Mary Sykes Wylie, "Why Is This Man Smiling?" *Psychotherapy Networker* (January/February, 2003).

6 In addition to the sources cited above on neural pathways, see Daniel Goleman, *Working with Emotional Intelligence* (Bantam Books, 1998).

Chapter Three

1 Many of the limiting beliefs that are listed here come from two sources: David Gershon and Gail Staub, *Empowerment* (High Point Press, 1989), and Phil McGraw, *Life Strategies* (Hyperion, 1999). Others have been contributed by people I have worked with over the years.

2 This method was created from information appearing in Debbie Ford, *Dark Side of the Light Chasers* (Riverhead Books, 1998) and Maryann Troiani and Michael Mercer, *Spontaneous Optimism* (Castlegate Publications, 1998).

3 The schemas presented here, as well as information on releasing faulty schemas, were derived from two sources: Jeffrey Young and Janet Klosko, *Reinventing Your Life*, (Plume, 1994) and C. Elliott and M. Lassen, *Why Can't I Get What I Want?* (Davies Black, 1998).

4 A good source of information on the amygdala and emotional hijacks is David Goleman, *Emotional Intelligence* (Bantam Books, 1997).

Chapter Four

[1] Steven Covey, in his book, *The 7 Habits of Highly Effective People*, discusses the importance of language as an indicator of being proactive. See also J. Perry, *The Road to Optimism* (Manfit Press, 1997) for a look at the use of language and its impact on optimistic attitudes.

[2] For more information on willpower and waypower, see C. R. Snyder, *The Psychology of Hope* (Free Press, 1994). Snyder focuses on the role of goals in obtaining and maintaining an attitude of hope.

Chapter Five

[1] See S. C. Vaughan, *Half Empty, Half Full* (Harcourt, 2000).

[2] For information on studies such as this, see Martin Seligman, *Authentic Happiness* (Free Press, 2002) and Daniel Goleman, *Emotional Intelligence* (Bantam Books, 1995).

[3] The concept and components described in this strategy are based on research on mental creativity. For more information, see M. Marskske and S. L. Willis, "Practical creativity in older adults' everyday problem solving: Life span perspectives," in C. E. Adams-Price (Ed.) *Creativity and Successful Aging* (Springer Publishing, 1998). This article is also the source for the brainstorming activity.

Chapter Six

[1] See Jeffrey Schwartz and Sharon Begley. *The Mind and The Brain: Neuroplasticity and the Power of Mental Force* (HarperCollins Publishers, 2002).

[2] The concept of perceptual position comes from work on Neuro-Linguistic Programming (NLP). For further information, see *www.nlpinfo.com*.

[3] The difference between intuition and impulse comes from Nancy Rosanoff, *Intuition Workout* (Aslan Publishers, 1991).

Chapter Seven

[1] The stories about John Irving and Harrison Ford were seen on the Bravo channel's shows "Inside the Actor's Studio" and "From Page to Screen." The Post-It® Note story can be found on numerous Web sites in various forms, and the information about Bill Walton comes from *Great Failures of the Extremely Successful* by Steve Young (Tallfellow Press, 2002).

[2] The notion of self-acceptance is discussed in detail in Nathaniel Branden's *The Six Pillars of Self-Esteem* (Bantam, 1994).

Chapter Eight

[1] For information on the study described here, see Emmy Werner and Ruth Smith, *Overcoming the Odds: High Risk Children from Birth to Adulthood* (Cornell University Press, 1992). For further information on this topic, visit *www.resiliency.com*.

[2] Explanatory styles are described in detail by Martin Seligman in *Learned Optimism* (Free Press, 1998). Seligman states that optimists explain their setbacks as being "non-personal." I prefer the term "not entirely personal" in keeping with the Proactive strategy of *Maintaining Personal Accountability*. POWER Optimists assess their role in any given setback and take the necessary corrective actions. The examples of setbacks are taken from Steve Young, *Great Failures of the Extremely Successful* (Tallfellow Press, 2002).

[3] This study was done by Dr. Robert Emmons, a professor of psychology at the University of California, Davis. For more information on his research, you can visit his Web site at *www.psychology.ucdavis.edu/labs/emmons*.

[4] In her book, *Emotional Alchemy: How the Mind Can Heal the Heart* (Harmony Books, 2001), Tara Bennett-Goleman describes in depth the process of observing feelings using mindful meditation.

[5] There is a great deal of information on logotherapy and Victor Frankl's teachings available on various Web sites.

[6] See M.S. Miles and E. Crandall, "The search for meaning and its potential for affecting growth in bereaved parents." *Health Issues*, Vol. 7, 1983, pp. 19-23.

About the Author

Dana Lightman, Ph.D., is a psychotherapist, coach, consultant and educator with 20 years experience. Dana specializes in the area of positive psychology, empowering clients to create the lives they want. As a dynamic training specialist, she has designed and conducted programs for corporations, hospitals, schools and universities. She has taught at the University of Pennsylvania and Temple University, appeared on radio and television and delivered keynote programs for conferences. She is a professional member of The National Speakers Association, an active member and past president of the Professionally Speaking Chapter of Toastmasters International and has studied dramatic presentation techniques at the Walnut and Wilma Theaters in Philadelphia, Pennsylvania.

Dana's mission is to release and increase the optimist in each of us with her POWER Optimism™ Programs. The programs are suitable for groups of all sizes and professions. For further information about POWER Optimism™ workshops, POWER Optimism™ At Work and speaking presentations, please visit *www.poweroptimism.com* or call 215-885-2127.

Contact Dr. Lightman with your POWER Optimism story:

Dana Lightman, Ph.D.
2464 Lafayette Avenue
Abington, PA 19001
215-885-2127
dana@poweroptimism.com